The International Trout and Salmon Cookbook

. . . they say Fish should swim thrice . . . first it should swim in the Sea; (do you mind me?) then it should swim in Butter; and at last Sirrah, it should swim in good Claret.

—*Jonathan Swift,* Polite Conversation

The International Trout and Salmon Cookbook

Gary J. McMaster, LL.B.

South Brunswick and New York: A. S. Barnes and Company
London: Thomas Yoseloff Ltd

© 1970 by A. S. Barnes and co., Inc.
Library of Congress Catalogue Card Number: 73-88285

A. S. Barnes and Co., Inc.
Cranbury, New Jersey 08512

Thomas Yoseloff Ltd
108 New Bond Street
London W1Y OQX, England

SBN: 498 07486 2
Printed in the United States of America

Contents

Preface

I wish it were possible for me to describe adequately all the pleasure that angling has provided me with over the years. If only everyone were able to take delight in the charms of the outdoors—the fields, the streams, the forests—as I have been able to. Even the hardships of the wild—the rugged trails, the bitter cold, the relentless swarms of insects, the sudden storms—have left their own abiding memories.

When the angler hears the wind rushing through the tall, sweet-smelling pines, the birds crying out from high above, the water tumbling and gurgling on its merry way, and the trout rising with a hearty splash, he forgets the difficulties which may beset his everyday existence, and feels a part of a much more comfortable and natural life.

When anglers huddle about the campfire at eventide, the steaming aromas come pouring from the coffeepot, the frying bacon, and the sizzling trout or salmon. The frigid wind sends the anglers closer to the fire, and they while away the remainder of the evening swapping stories about the half hour spent playing and finally landing (or losing) the big one, about slipping on the mossy rocks and kissing the cold drink, and about what flies or lures they've found most successful in particular spots.

That's what an angler's memories are made of.

Like anything else, cooking fish can be as simple or as complicated as you care to make it. But trout and salmon, properly prepared, provide some of the finest in gourmet dining, whether you are seated at a candle-lit, damask-covered table and eating with golden dinnerware, or squatting beside a sputtering campfire in the Yukon and eating with your fingers. Having experienced both, I can assure you of the truth of that statement.

To cook fish well, however, you must keep uppermost in mind two things: first of all, trout and salmon, like any fish, is a highly perishable food—therefore the fresher the better. Second, it must not be overcooked, or it will be tough and dry.

Over the years, I have gathered these recipes from around the globe. They come from practically wherever trout and salmon come from, and I believe they are the best. So just allow me to wish you much fishing fun (if you are inclined toward the art) and a great deal of eating enjoyment!

G. J. M.

English Equivalent Measures

	American	English
1 cup of breadcrumbs (fresh)	1½ oz.	3 oz.
1 cup of flour or other powdered grains	4 oz.	5 oz.
1 cup of sugar	7 oz.	8 oz.
1 cup of icing sugar	4½ oz.	5 oz.
1 cup of butter or other fats	8 oz.	8 oz.
1 cup of raisins, etc.	5 oz.	6 oz.
1 cup of grated cheese	4 oz.	4 oz.
1 cup of syrup, etc.	12 oz.	14 oz.

1 English pint	20 fluid ounces
1 American pint	16 fluid ounces
1 American cup	8 fluid ounces
8 American tablespoons	4 fluid ounces
1 American tablespoon	½ fluid ounce
3 American teaspoons	½ fluid ounce
1 English tablespoon	⅔ to 1 fluid ounce (approx.)
1 English tablespoon	4 teaspoons

The American measuring tablespoon holds ¼ oz. flour

The International Trout and Salmon Cookbook

1

Preparing the Trout or Salmon

When you first catch your fish—or, if less fortunate, when you first bring it home from the market—remove the scales. To scale your fish, hold it firmly near the tail and scrape the scales downward toward the head, using a scaling knife or the back of a regular knife. Some find a sharp-edged tablespoon satisfactory for scaling medium-sized fish. It is always easier to scale a fish when it is wet than when it is dry, so you can simplify the work by soaking your fish in cold water for a few minutes before beginning. Be certain to remove all the scales around the base of the fins and head. If the fish is under a pound, however, there is no need to remove the scales at all, as they aren't big enough to worry about.

With a sharp knife, cut the entire length of the belly from the vent (anal opening) to the head, and remove the entrails without breaking them. Be sure to remove the heavy vein that runs along the backbone. Wash the fish immediately in cold water, drain, and wipe off excess moisture.

Removing the head and tail is optional. Some people think that fish cooked with the head and tail on are more moist. This is the way I prefer mine. Not only does the fish look more impressive with the head, but it serves a practical purpose as well: when the eyes turn white, you know that the fish is done. If you like your fish this way, just wash in cold running water after cleaning, remove any excess membrane or viscera, and you're ready for business.

If, however, you are one who either does not like to fool with the head and fins while eating, or you just cannot stand looking the fish in the eye while you're cooking him, here are the proper procedures for the complete dressing or filleting of your fish, whether it be trout or salmon.

DRESSING: Cut above collarbone, removing the head. If removal of the head is made difficult by a large backbone, just cut

13

through to the backbone on each side of the fish just above the collarbone. Then place the fish on the edge of the table so that the head hangs over, and snap the backbone by bending the head down. Cut off any remaining flesh that holds the head to the body and remove the pectoral fins (on either side, just back of the gills). Next, cut off the tail. To remove the large dorsal fin on the back of the fish, cut around it at its base and give it a quick pull toward the head, removing the fin and its root bones. Remove the ventral fins (on the underside, in back) in the same manner. Wash your fish off in cold running water now, and if it is a large fish you may now cut it crossways into steaks.

FILLETING: If your object is to make fillets from your whole fish, first scale if necessary, then follow this procedure: with a sharp knife, cut through the flesh along the back from the tail to just behind the head. Next, cut down to the backbone just above the collarbone. Turn the knife flat and cut the flesh along the backbone all the way to the tail, lifting the entire side of the fish away in one piece. Turn the fish over and repeat on the other side.

SKINNING: If you wish to skin your fillets, lay them one at a time on the cutting board or table, skin side down. With one hand, hold the tail and tightly to the table. With your knife in the other hand, cut through the flesh to the skin about half an inch from the tail end. Flatten the knife on the skin and cut the flesh away by pushing the knife forward toward the head end.

If you have a revolving spit with your outdoor grill or in front of your fireplace, it is no trick to spit and roast either a whole large trout or a salmon, and it is a particular treat for the eyes as well as for the palate. Merely make slits in the skin of the fish, and slip into them slivers of garlic and fat bacon, and herbs such as thyme and rosemary. Impale the fish on the spit and tie thin slices of bacon around it. These will then melt with cooking and protect the flesh. Keep the fish in shape by tying it with string and basting frequently with the cooking juices.

Although many of the recipes here may specify a particular type of trout or salmon, it is usually because that species is native to the area where the recipe originated, and in most cases any species is suitable. Also, large trout can often be prepared according to many of the salmon recipes, so do not always feel tied to the specific fish suggested.

2
Outdoor Cooking Methods

Many times, in various wilds of the world, I have found myself with an insatiable hunger for my catch, but no skillet. On the following page, I have illustrated and explained the best methods I have found to fill this void, as old-time woodsmen and Indians did.

If you want your outdoor-broiled salmon or trout to come out with an especially delicious flavor, brush it frequently all during the cooking process with bacon fat or Argentine Chuqui. (Part III)

ON A POLE (Illustrations *a* and *b*): For a salmon or large trout. Remove head and tail, scale, clean and wash. Select a long green hardwood bough, strip it of bark, and place it over the fire or coals by means of stick supports, as in illustration *a*, or large rocks, as in *b*. It is best to truss the fish securely to the pole with leader wire or something similar, so that it stays in place and you can turn it upside down to cook it more evenly. When it appears to be done, remove from the heat and test it with your knife to see if it flakes easily.

TLINGIT INDIAN STYLE (Illustration *c*): This is how the Tlingits, the northernmost tribe of Pacific Coast Indians, have always broiled their salmon. For salmon or large trout. Clean, wash and fillet. Cut two straight boughs of alder or willow about twenty inches longer than the fillets. Split each bough at the thick end and place one fillet between the split. Cut and strip four small sticks and place two criss-cross on each side of the fillet (between the fish and the bough) to hold the fillet flat. Pull the end of the split closed and tie together tight with strips of bark, rawhide, or what have you. Stick the end of the bough into the ground close enough to the fire for the fish to cook, but not so close that it burns. Cook until well done, turning when necessary. When the fillet is done, cut the twine and slide it out, keeping it held between the four smaller sticks. If you have such civilized products avail-

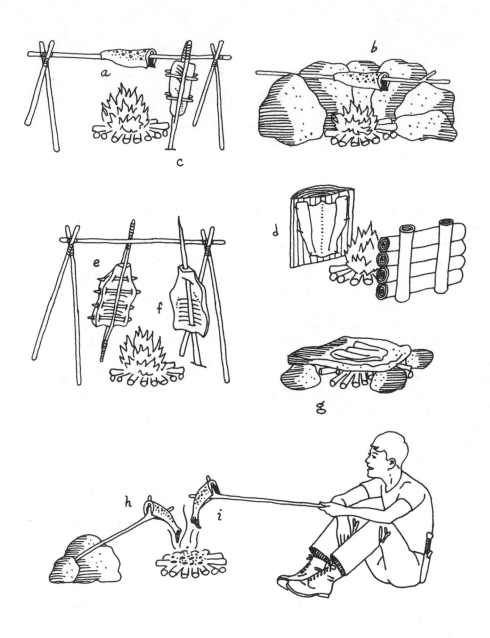

able, you can salt and pepper to taste, or even dip into melted butter.

ON A PLANK (Illustration *d*) : For salmon or large trout. Clean the fish by cutting off the head and tail, scaling it, then slitting it down the back from end to end, removing dorsal fin. Now spread it open, leaving the belly intact, so that it is in a butterfly shape. Clean it of all entrails, wash and dry it. Take a short clean plank of hardwood, or a short split log, and tack the fish, skin side down, to the wood, using nails or sharp green hardwood pegs, stripped of bark. Set the fish near the fire, as shown in the illustration, propping it if necessary. You may have to adjust the plank before the fire occasionally to be certain that the fish broils evenly at the proper heat. The cooking time will be from 20 to 30 minutes, depending on the heat and the size of the fish. When the flesh flakes from the skin, add salt and pepper and serve it from the plank. Your fish will broil better if you set up a reflector on the opposite side of the fire to direct more heat onto the fish. Build the reflector either with logs, as in the illustration, or with rocks, on the order of illustration *b*.

ON SKEWERS (Illustrations *e* and *f*) : For salmon or large trout. Fillet the fish and skewer each fillet on four or five sharpened green hardwood sticks, stripped of bark, as in illustration *e*. Then split a green hardwood bough a couple of feet longer than your fillet. Slip the fillet in and bind both ends of the split bough with strips of bark, rawhide, or what have you. (Or try just running the sapling stick directly through the fillet as in illustration *f*.) Lean the skewer against a horizontal bar or other support, as in *e* or else merely stick it into the ground, as in *f*. Turn the fillets occasionally so that they broil evenly; they should be done in about 30 minutes.

ON A ROCK (Illustration *g*) : Select a large flat rock (it must be dry, of course), and heat it over a fire as shown in the illustration. Or, if your fire is big enough, put the rock *in* the fire instead of over it. In the meantime, clean the fish by cutting off the head and tail, scaling if necessary, then slitting it down the back from end to end, removing dorsal fin. Now spread it open, leaving the belly intact, in butterfly shape. Clean it of entrails, wash and dry it. If your rock was in the fire, push it out when it's good and hot and leaves or an evergreen bough to brush it clean. Then set your butterfly fillets on the rock, skin side down. Add a little salt and pepper, if available, and some butter or bacon. Let the fillet or fillets bake on the hot rock until the flesh flakes easily. The skin will stick to the rock, so the rock will serve as your plate, too.

ON A STICK (Illustrations *h* and *i*) : For small trout. Clean, remove head, and scale if necessary. Select a sturdy green hardwood sapling bough with a good fork on the end, and strip it of bark. Stick the fork into the fish in two places, so that it is securely pinned. Hold it over the coals or fire, as in illustration *i*, or else prop it up with rocks, as in *h*, until it flakes easily.

IN A TRENCH (Not illustrated) : One additional way to prepare a large trout or salmon is this method, which has long been popular among steelhead and salmon fishermen. These directions are best suited for a large freshly-caught trout or salmon of about 20 pounds. To begin with, you must dig a trench in the gravel or sandy soil wide enough and long enough to accommodate your fish, and about four inches deep.

Three or four hours before cooking the fish, build a roaring fire in the trench. Pile the driftwood high enough so that the heat thoroughly permeates the soil for at least a foot beneath the bottom of the trench.

To prepare the fish itself, first brush it liberally with olive oil, inside and out, and salt and pepper it generously. Next, roll the whole fish into three to seven layers of heavy parchment, such as unwaxed butcher paper, and fold over the ends.

Now, dig out about six inches of the hot gravel or sand from the trench and place the wrapped fish in the bottom. Quickly recover the fish with sand, and rebuild the fire on top of it. Keep the fire going great guns for six to eight hours. (With practice, of course, you can determine the exact time that best suits the soil and weather conditions of your particular locale).

Be careful when removing the fish from the trench, as the paper will have become dry and weak. A flattering accompaniment is the "4 B's—Bread, Butter, Beer and Baked potatoes.

Part I
Trout

Introduction

A brace of wild mountain trout, fresh-caught from a cold stream in the High Sierras, cooked with bacon over a crackling campfire . . . the combined flavors of wood smoke, bacon, and the delicate trout could not be duplicated, even in an ultramodern kitchen by the most experienced European chef. However, the utmost sophistication can work its particular miracles with trout just as outdoor simplicity can. Anyone who has ever sampled Trout Amandine at the Restaurant Casenave, or Truite en chemise at the station resturant in the Gare de l'Est in Paris, can swear to that. But you don't have to go halfway around the world to enjoy these exquisite dishes—you can enjoy them in your own home, provided you can follow the few simple directions.

Many of the recipes here are for the small trout—rainbows, browns, and brook char—running from about eight inches to a foot. If the trout you intend to cook is one of the larger varieties, such as steelhead, kamloops, or lack char, there are recipes especially for these too, either whole or sliced. You will find also, as suggested before, that many of the salmon recipes work very well with large trout.

Of course, the simplest way to prepare a big trout is simply to remove the bones and skin, cut the trout into fillets, bread them, and fry them until golden brown. Then serve with Sauce Tartare and cole slaw.

3
Sautéed Trout

Trout Sautéed Streamside

If you catch trout early and can have them for breakfast that same morning, consider yourself among the most fortunate of mortals.

To cook a half dozen trout, first fry 6 to 12 strips of bacon, depending on your appetite. When the bacon is crisp, remove it to a paper or plate. Dip the cleaned trout in flour or corn meal and sauté them quickly in the bacon fat. Do not add salt until the fish are cooked and you have tasted them, for the bacon fat may add enough seasoning. Serve the trout with the bacon strips and toast made over the fire. Steaming campfire coffee, of course, is a "must."

Trout Sauté À La Meunière

This is the preferred method of cookery for small whole fish rather than for fillets or steaks. However, if you wish to cook fillets or steaks this way, there is no "rule" against it. And they will taste very good.

The trout is not coated, merely seasoned with salt and pepper (if possible, about an hour or so ahead of time). Obviously, careful attention is needed to prevent the fish from sticking to the pan or breaking when it is turned.

Add clarified butter to your skillet. When it is hot but not burned, add the fish and sauté until nicely browned on one side. Turn and brown the other side.

This is accompanied by *beurre noisette*: simply put butter into a hot pan and cook it over a moderate fire until it is a delicate nut-brown. Add lemon juice or lime juice if desired. It is essential to use fresh butter and a clean pan when preparing the *beurre noi-*

22

sette, and to pour it over the trout as soon as the butter is foaming and the color of a pale hazelnut, as the French name implies.

It is no use attempting preparation à la meunière unless you are prepared to be meticulous, have a sufficiently large pan to hold all the fish at one time, and an audience ready to eat it the moment you whisk it to the table.

VARIATION: You may, if you like, dip your cleaned fish in milk and roll in flour prior to sautéing; and just before removing them from the pan, add ½ to 1 cup of heavy cream. Let it come to a boil and cook for 2 minutes. Remove the trout to a hot platter. Correct the seasoning, reduce the cream a bit, and pour it over the fish. Sprinkle with chopped parsley.

Trout A L'Anglaise

12 small trout
2 eggs
2 cups crumbs
4 tablespoons butter
3 tablespoons olive oil
Flour
Salt and pepper

Clean and wash the trout. Beat the eggs lightly, and crush or roll the crumbs.

Heat the butter and olive oil in a large skillet. Dust the trout with flour, sprinkle with salt and pepper, dip in the egg, and then in the crumbs. Sauté in the hot fat until golden brown. Remove to a hot platter and serve with Sauce Tartare or Sauce Remoulade (Part III). Boiled potatoes and peas are a good accompaniment.

Trout In Marinade Sauce

First prepare trout:
6 medium trout
Salt and pepper
Flour
Olive oil

Clean and wash trout, removing heads and fins. Season with salt and pepper. Roll in flour and fry evenly in olive oil, or mixture of olive oil and salad oil, for 10 to 15 minutes. Do not let oil get brown. When done, remove the trout to another pan. Drain off excess oil.

Now make marinade sauce in the pan in which the fish were fried:

1 can beef or chicken broth
Juice of 1 lemon
½ teaspoon rosemary leaves
2 bay leaves
1 teaspoon prepared mustard
½ cup dry wine
Salt
Pinch of cayenne pepper
3 tablespoons vinegar
1 teaspoon savory
3 egg yolks

Combine all ingredients, except eggs, in the frying pan and boil for 15 minutes. Strain through a cloth. Whip eggs in a bowl. Pour hot broth slowly into eggs, whipping while you pour. Reheat. When sauce comes to a boil, pour over pan of fish. There should be enough sauce to cover them. Delicious either hot or cold.

Truite En Chemise

First, prepare 6 crepes (French pancakes) without sugar. They should be about 6 inches in diameter, well browned, thin and tender:

¾ cup sifted enriched flour
½ teaspoon salt
¾ cup milk
3 eggs, slightly beaten

Mix flour and salt. Add milk alternately with eggs. Beat until smooth. Grease bottom of heavy frying pan when very hot. Cover bottom of pan with thin layer of batter and quickly tilt pan so that the pancake is evenly paper-thin. Brown on both sides. Successful making of crepes depends upon the thinness of the batter.

Now prepare the following:
½ pound mushrooms
4 tablespoons butter

Salt and pepper
3 tablespoons flour
4 tablespoons heavy cream

Chop the mushrooms very fine. Sauté them in the butter until they are soft and well cooked. Sprinkle with salt, pepper, and flour. Add the heavy cream and stir until the mixture is thick. Set aside.

Now your trout:
6 medium trout
Browned butter
Lemon juice

Clean and wash the trout, then sauté them à la meunière, according to directions in chapter 3. Now spread each crepe with the mushroom mixture, place a trout on top of this and roll up the pancake so that the head sticks out at one end and the tail out the other. Arrange these rolls in a baking dish, cover with a little *beurre noisette,* and heat for a moment or two in the oven. Serve with a crisp green salad and a brittle white wine.

Trout Amandine

4 medium trout
½ pound shelled almonds
6 tablespoons butter
Flour
Salt and pepper
Chopped parsley

Clean and wash the trout. Blanch the almonds. Leave half of them whole and cut the rest into slivers. Melt the butter in a skillet. Dip the trout in flour, and when the butter is bubbly but not burning, add the trout and the almonds. Spoon the nuts around in the butter so they will brown well. Turn the trout once—they will take only a few minutes to cook. Salt and pepper to taste. Remove the trout to a hot platter and sprinkle with chopped parsley. Pour the golden-colored almonds and the butter from the pan over the trout. Serve along with small baked potatoes. If you like, add some lemon or lime butter (simply heat the amount of butter desired and add lemon or lime juice to taste), or lemon or lime wedges.

Rio Maule Trout Sauté

8 medium trout
1 teaspoon salt
1 teaspoon pepper
2 cups milk
8 tablespoons flour
4 tablespoon olive oil
1 cup fine bread crumbs
2 tablespoons capers, chopped
Juice of 1 lemon
1 ripe avocado

Clean and wash the trout. Sprinkle them with salt and pepper, dip them in milk, then roll them in flour and cook them in the heated olive oil on both sides until they are crisply golden. Drain olive oil from pan and discard. Put fish on a hot platter and keep warm. Melt the butter in the pan in which the fish browned, stir in bread crumbs and cook them, stirring, until they also are brown. Sprinkle the capers over the trout. Then pour on the lemon juice and cover with bread crumbs and butter. Garnish each trout with a slice of avocado.

Austrian Brown Trout In Cream

6 medium brown trout
½ teaspoon salt
½ teaspoon pepper
2 cups milk
1 cup flour
6 tablespoons butter
2½ tablespoons brandy
2 cups heavy cream
2 tablespoons slivered almonds, browned in butter

Clean and wash the trout. Sprinkle with salt and pepper, dip in milk, roll in flour and brown on both sides in melted butter. Warm the brandy, pour over trout and set aflame. When flame dies, stir in heavy cream and bring to a simmer. Remove trout to hot platter and keep warm. Cook sauce, stirring often, until it is thickened and all particles in the pan are well blended with the cream. Strain, pour over the fish. Sprinkle buttered almonds over trout and serve.

Trout Fillets Milanese

1¼ cups fresh-cooked trout, boned, skinned, and chopped
2 tablespoon flour
1 tablespoon Cream of Wheat
2 eggs yolks
½ teaspoon salt
½ teaspoon pepper
¼ teaspoon nutmeg
2 cups milk
1 tablespoon grated Parmesan cheese
½ cup flour
1 egg, slightly beaten
1 cup bread crumbs
1 cup olive oil
1 lemon, cut into wedges

Mix together flour, Cream of Wheat, egg yolks, salt pepper, nutmeg and milk. Place on fire and cook until thickened, stirring constantly. Add trout flesh to Parmesan cheese, mixing well. Pour over well-floured board and spread 1 inch thick. Cut into slices 2 inches wide and 4 inches long. Flour slices well, dip into egg, roll in bread crumbs, and fry in hot oil until golden brown on both sides. Serve with lemon wedges. Serves four.

Sicilian-Style Trout Sauté

½ cup olive oil
1 teaspoon salt
4 small trout
1 teaspoon diced sweet red peppers
½ lemon, cut into wedges

Heat olive oil in frying pan, add salt and sweet peppers, and let oil become very hot. Add trout, cover pan, and cook 15 minutes on each side. Serve with lemon wedges.

Down East Brook Trout

Salt pork, an old New England favorite, imparts unique flavor to a delicate fish:

½ pound lean salt pork
6 medium brook trout
½ cup yellow corn meal

1 teaspoon salt
½ teaspoon paprika
Sauce Tartare
Parsley or watercress

Cut salt pork into 6 even slices. Sauté slowly in a large heavy frying pan, turning often, until crisp. Remove and drain on paper towels, keeping warm.

Clean trout and wash in lightly salted cold water. Pat dry. Mix corn meal, salt, and paprika in a large shallow pan. Roll trout in mixture, coating evenly. Fry trout slowly in pork drippings for 4 minutes. Turn and cook 3 to 4 minutes longer, or until fish is golden and flakes easily with a fork.

Arrange trout and browned salt pork on a hot serving platter. Pour Sauce Tartare over them and garnish with parsley or watercress.

Steelhead Florentine Sauté

4 steelhead steaks
Flour
4 tablespoons butter
Salt and pepper
3 cups finely chopped spinach
1 clove garlic
1 teaspoon tarragon
Juice of 1 lemon

Dip the steaks in flour and sauté in butter until done. Season with salt and pepper to taste. Serve steaks on a bed of chopped cooked spinach which has been flavored with garlic, tarragon, and lemon juice. Surround with slices of boiled potato browned in butter and mixed with sliced mushrooms.

Truite Grenobloise

4 medium trout
Salt and pepper
Salt butter
Flour
½ teaspoon finely chopped garlic
2 tablespoons finely chopped shallot
1 small cucumber, peeled, seeded and finely diced
3 firm tomatoes, skinned, seeded, and shredded
    (reserve seeds)

 >

2 limes, peeled, sectioned, and diced
3 lemons, peeled, sectioned, and diced
Lemon slices
1 tablespoon chopped fresh parsley

Clean and wash trout, and dry with a cloth. Season the inside of each trout with salt and pepper and put in a little butter. Reshape and dust with flour. Heat 1½ ounces salt butter in a pan and cook the fish slowly on each side. Remove; arrange on a hot flat serving dish. Add to the pan the chopped garlic and shallot, cucumber, tomatoes, and the lime and lemon sections. Rub the tomato seeds through a strainer and add to the mixture. Season with salt and pepper, cover pan and cook slowly for 3 minutes. Carefully pour this mixture over the trout, surround with lemon slices and sprinkle with parsley. Serves four.

Truites À La Mode de Héas (Pyrenees Style)

First prepare a Duxelles:
4 ounces mushroom stalks and trimmings
¼ medium onion, chopped
½ ounce butter
1½ tablespoons olive oil
1 chopped shallot
Salt and pepper
⅛ teaspoon grated nutmeg

Chop up the mushrooms stalks and trimmings finely, and squeeze them in a cloth by twisting it, so that as much of their moisture as possible is extracted. Lightly brown the onion in the combined butter and olive oil, add the shallot, mushrooms, salt and pepper to taste, and nutmeg. Stir on a hot fire until all the moisture in the mushrooms has evaporated. Pour the Duxelles into a bowl, press it down lightly, and keep it covered with a buttered paper until ready for use.

Next, the trout:
6 trout (about 5 oz. each)
Salt and pepper
Flour
Clarified butter
Hard-boiled eggs
Parsley, chopped
Beurre noisette

Season and flour trout, and sauté them in clarified butter. Spread the Duxelles on a serving dish, arrange trout on it, and sprinkle them generously with chopped yolk of hot hard-boiled egg mixed with chopped parsley. Sprinkle with *beurre noisette* (see Trout Sauté à la Meunière), using about an ounce of butter for each trout. The dish should be served as quickly as possible so that the butter is still foaming when it comes to the table.

Siamese Trout With Ginger Sauce

1 3-pound trout
Vegetable oil
Salted flour
Parsley sprigs

Clean and wash trout and rub generously with oil. Dredge in salted flour, and fry in ¼ inch of hot oil until golden brown on both sides (about 3 to 5 minutes). Drain on absorbent paper.

Serve with the following ginger sauce poured over it:
3 tablespons minced fresh or crystallized ginger
¼ cup sugar
¼ cup vingear
1 tablespoon soy sauce
1 cup water
Salt
¼ cup chopped mushrooms
¼ cup chopped scallions, both green and phite parts
1 teaspoon cornstarch, dissolved in 1 tablespoon water

Combine ginger, sugar, vinegar, soy sauce, water, salt, and simmer for 10 minutes. Add mushrooms and scallions and cook a few minutes longer or until mushrooms are tender. Stir in cornstarch paste and simmer a minute or so until sauce thickens. Serve immediately over trout and garnish with parsley.

4
Baked Trout

Stuffed Large Trout

You will often hear fishermen say, "I like the small trout best. They taste better. I don't care for the big ones. They don't have a good flavor." More often than not, however, this is a simple case of sour grapes: he's using that as an excuse because he didn't *catch* any big ones. All such rationalizations aside, you will often find that the bigger the trout the bigger the flavor. Providing, of course, that it is prepared correctly. One of the best ways to prepare a large trout is by stuffing and baking it. Have the fish boned by someone who knows how to remove bones leaving the skin intact. The scales have to be removed first.

Prepare the following stuffing:
1 onion, minced
3 stalks celery, minced
¾ cup cooked shrimp, sliced
1 tablespoon chopped parsley
1 egg, beaten
Juice of ½ lemon
¼ cup sweet or sour cream
Salt and pepper
Cracker crumbs

Fry the onion and celery, then mix with the other ingredients, using enough cracker crumbs to bind them together. Stuff the trout. Bake with a sauce of your choice, or topped with strips of bacon, in a 350-degree oven for 30 to 45 minutes. Figure about two servings per pound.

31

Stuffed Shirt Trout

This is a very dressy stuffed trout—a spectacular dish for special occasions.

    12 medium trout
    2 medium onions
    Butter
    Salt and pepper
    ½ pound raw white-meated fish
    2 egg yolks
    3 egg whites
    Chopped tarragon
    Chopped parsley
    3 large onions
    6 tablespoons butter
    2 cups dry white wine
    1 cup very heavy Sauce Bechamel
    ½ pound butter

Clean and wash trout, leaving heads intact.

Chop the onions and sauté them in butter until they are soft and golden. Salt them lightly. Grind the white-meated fish several times, and salt and pepper it to taste. Add it to the onions and blend the two together with a wooden spoon. Add the egg yolks and egg whites, slightly beaten, and season with tarragon and parsley. Stuff the fish with this mixture.

Chop 3 large onions and sauté them in 6 tablespoons of butter until soft. Force them through a sieve or food mill. Cover the bottom of a baking dish with this onion puree and arrange the trout on top. Dot them with butter, add the wine, and bake in a 450-degree oven for 8 to 10 minutes, just until the fish are cooked.

Remove the fish to a hot platter. Force the sauce through a sieve or food mill and combine it with 1 cup of very heavy Bechamel and ½ pound of butter. Blend thoroughly and pour over the fish. Sprinkle with chopped parsley. Serve with julienne potatoes and a crisp green salad.

Baked Trout Creole

Begin by preparing Creole Sauce:

    2 medium onions, sliced
    3 green peppers, sliced

1 clove garlic, crushed
½ cup butter or bacon drippings
2 cups canned tomatoes
1 cup water
1 can onion soup
Juice of 1 lemon

Braise onions, green pepper, and garlic in butter or bacon drippings until almost brown. Add all other ingredients but lemon juice.
Cook very slowly for 1 hour.

In the meantime, prepare trout:
4 medium trout
Salt and pepper
Flour
Olive oil
Can of mushroom soup
1½ cans cream or milk
Oregano
Parsley, chopped

Clean and wash trout. Season with salt and pepper, coat thinly
with flour, and sauté in olive oil until browned on both sides. Place
in baking pan. Add mushroom soup, diluted with 1½ cans of cream
or milk. Bake in 350-degree oven for about 30 minutes, basting
frequently.

When both fish and Creole Sauce are done, add juice of 1 lemon
to hot sauce and pour over trout. Sprinkle with oregano and parsley.

Trout Baked In Red Wine

First, you must sacrifice one trout before you start the cooking
and make a fish stock, thus:

1 medium trout
2 small white onions, thinly sliced
3 sprigs parsley
6 peppercorns
3 cups water
3 cups white wine
1 teaspoon salt

Clean, wash, and chop trout. Put fish, including head and bones,
into pot with onions, parsley, and peppercorns. Pour in half a cup
of water. Cover pot and simmer for 20 minutes. Now add the rest

of the water and the wine and salt and cook for another 25 minutes. Strain and set aside.

Next, the following are required to cook the trout:

    1 large buttered casserole
    8 white onions, minced
    8 medium trout
    2 cups red wine
    2 cups fish stock
    1 sprig parsley
    6 peppercorns
    Sheet of heavy waxed paper, heavily buttered

Clean and wash trout. Arrange the onions in the buttered casserole, place the trout over them, and add the red wine and the fish stock. The fish should be half-covered. Add the parsley and peppercorns. Bring the casserole contents to a boil on top of the stove. Remove from fire, cover snugly with the buttered paper and bake in a preheated 300-degree oven for 15 minutes, remembering that the liquid around the fish should be just a-simmer, not boiling violently. Baste several times with a bulb-type baster.

Now place the trout on a hot serving dish. Keep them warm. Strain the liquid in which they were cooked, put it in a saucepan, and cook over a high flame, stirring constantly so that it doesn't burn. When sauce is reduced by half, pour over the trout and serve immediately.

Trota Con Prosciutto

    6 medium trout
    ½ teaspoon salt
    ½ teaspoon pepper
    6 slices Italian ham
    ½ cup heavy cream
    4 tablespoons finely chopped chives

Clean and wash the trout. Sprinkle with salt and pepper, place in a deep buttered casserole and cover each trout with a very thin slice of the ham. Bake in 350-degree oven for 15 minutes. Pour in the cream and bake for 10 minutes more, basting several times. Dot with chives and serve from the dish at the table, accompanied by broiled tomato halves. Add a side dish of watercress cooked in chicken broth—and don't forget the white vino.

Kings Canyon Barbecue

6 medium trout
Salt and pepper
Flour
Olive oil
⅓ cup dry white wine
1/3 cup barbecue sauce
Juice of 1 lemon
Oregano

Clean and wash the trout. Season with salt and pepper. Coat thinly with flour. Fry in oil until half done, about 10 minutes. Place in a baking pan. Mix wine diluted with 2 tablespoons of water, barbecue sauce, and lemon juice. Baste the fish before placing in a 375-degree oven, and baste twice while baking. Fish will be done in about 30 minutes. Sprinkle with oregano and serve hot. Trout prepared this way are also delicious cold.

Brown Trout In Mushrooms

8 medium trout
1 pound mushrooms
6 tablespoons butter
1 clove garlic
1 teaspoon salt
1 teaspoon freshly ground black pepper
1½ cups (and 2 tablespoons) heavy cream
Butter
Beurre manière
Fried toast
Parsley

Clean and wash the trout. Chop the mushrooms very fine and sauté them in butter until they are soft. Season with minced garlic, salt and pepper. Add 2 tablespoons of cream and let it cook down.

Arrange trout in a well-oiled baking dish and top them with the mushrooms. Dot with butter and bake in a 425-degree oven for 10 minutes, or until the fish are just cooked through. Remove them to a hot platter. Add 1½ cups of heavy cream to the pan, heat, and blend thoroughly. Add *beurre manière* (make by kneading 2 tablespoons of butter with 3 tablespoons of flour) and stir until nicely thickened. Taste for seasoning and pour over the trout. Garnish the platter with pieces of fried toast heavily sprinkled with chopped parsley.

Gold Pavilion Trout

First, the trout:
4 medium trout
Salt and pepper
Fine Bread crumbs
Peanut oil
Sesame seeds

Clean and wash trout. Season with salt and pepper. Roll in crumbs and sesame seeds, and fry in peanut oil until browned, turning once. When done, trout will be tender and flaky when tested with a fork. Remove from the pan and cool until trout can be handled easily.

Meanwhile, prepare the Oriental Herb Sauce:
1 cup tomato juice
1/3 cup dry wine
6 water chestnuts, sliced
1 tablespoon sugar
1 tablespoon soy sauce
2 tablespoons chopped parsley
2 tablespoons tomato paste
1 can onion soup
1/3 teaspoon thyme
2 ounces bean sprouts, drained

Boil ingredients until of a suitable consistency.

Split trout open down the back and pull out bones. Close the back and place in baking pan. Pour Herb Sauce over trout. Bake in 350-degree oven for 10 minutes.

Remove to platter, sprinkle with diced leeks and garnish with whole parsley. Serve with side dishes of fancy mixed Chinese vegetables (available canned). Add individual cups of rice wine, and you have a rich reminder of the imperial splendor of old China.

Trout En Papillote

First, prepare the filling:
2 carrots
2 small white onions
2 shallots or green onions
2 stalks celery
4 to 6 tablespoons butter
Salt and pepper

Chop the vegetables fine and sauté them in the butter until soft. Salt and pepper to taste.

Now the trout:
6 medium trout
Butter
Salt and pepper
Oil

Clean and wash the trout, and inside each one put a little of the filling. Dot with butter, and place about 3 inches from the broiler flame, broiling for 4 minutes. Salt and pepper trout when you remove them.

Have ready 6 heart-shaped pieces of cooking parchment large enough for the trout. Place a fish on each piece of parchment, near one edge. Fold the rest of the paper over the fish and crimp the edges together so that the fish is sealed in. Oil the paper. Place these on a buttered baking sheet and bake in a 425-degree oven until the parchment is inflated and browned. Serve wrapped in paper.

Trout Souffle With Egg Sauce

1½ tablespoons butter
1 tablespoon flour
½ cup milk
2 egg yolks
2 cups trout flesh, boned, skinned and chopped
2 egg whites
1 cup heavy cream
Salt and pepper

Melt butter, mix in flour, and stir and cook until mixture is free of lumps. Add milk gradually and stir and cook mixture until it is smooth and thick. Remove from heat and beat egg yolks. Cool. Mash trout and fold into sauce. Season with salt and pepper. Beat egg white until fluffy and firm and then fold gently into fish mixture. Put in a greased baking dish and place dish in a pan with an inch of water in the bottom. Bake in a 350-degree oven until soufflé puffs up high and browns on top.

While soufflé is baking, prepare the Sauce Oeuf Dur (hard-boiled-egg sauce):

2 tablespoons butter
2 tablespoons flour

2 cups milk
1 teaspoon prepared mustard
2 hard-boiled eggs, chopped fine
1 teaspoon Worcestershire sauce
2 tablespoons lemon juice
1 tablespoon chopped parsley
Salt and pepper

Melt the butter in a pot and stir in flour. Mix until smooth and stir in milk gradually. Cook and stir until sauce becomes smooth and thick. Add mustard, chopped hard-boiled eggs, Worcestershire sauce, lemon juice, and chopped parsley. Season with salt and pepper.

When soufflé is done, pour sauce over it and serve immediately. This recipe also works especially fine with salmon.

Baked Trout Savoy

4 medium trout
¼ teaspoon salt
½ teaspoon pepper
½ cup flour
½ cup butter
1 tablespoon olive oil
1 tablespoon butter
½ pound mushrooms, sliced
¼ teaspoon salt
¼ teaspoon pepper
1 teaspoon minced parsley
1½ tablespoons fine bread crumbs
2 tablespoons butter, melted
¼ cup butter
1 scallion, minced

Clean and wash trout and sprinkle with salt and pepper. Roll in flour and fry in ½ cup butter slowly 10 minutes on each side, or until well done. Fry mushrooms in 1 tablespoon butter and oil for 10 minutes and add salt, pepper and parsley. Spread mushrooms in baking dish and place trout over them. Sprinkle with butter in which trout was sautéed and with bread crumbs. Sprinkle with 2 tablespoons melted butter and bake in 375-degree oven for 5 minutes. Heat ¼ cup butter, add minced scallion and simmer for 1 minute. Pour over fish and serve.

Baked Trout, Sicilian Style

8 medium trout fillets
1 large onion, chopped
1 tablespoon olive oil
1 medium can peeled tomatoes
½ cup water
3 cloves
½ teaspoon salt
½ teaspoon pepper
1 tablespoon flour
1 tablespoon water
12 green olives, pitted and chopped
1 tablespoon chopped parsley
2 tablespoons capers
1 stalk celery, minced

Brown onion in olive oil, add tomatoes, water, cloves, salt and pepper, cover pan and simmer for 20 minutes. Blend to smooth paste the flour and 1 tablespoon water, stir into tomato mixture and cook for 5 minutes. Add olives, parsley, capers and celery.

Place fish in greased baking dish, pour the tomato sauce over it and bake in 375-degree oven for 35 minutes, basting occasionally. Serve hot with sauce.

Steamed Rainbow

1 large rainbow trout
½ teaspoon salt
½ teaspoon pepper
¼ cup butter
1 small onion, chopped fine
1 small carrot, chopped fine
1 stalk celery, chopped fine
1 teaspoon minced parsley
¼ teaspoon thyme
½ bay leaf, minced
2 cups extra dry red wine, heated
2 teaspoons butter
½ tablespoon flour
½ cup light cream
¼ cup butter

Clean and wash trout. Sprinkle with salt and pepper, inside and out. Thoroughly butter a roasting pan with a cover. Place the onion, celery, parsley, thyme, and bay leaf in the roasting pan and place the trout over this. Add a little more butter, cover trout with greased paper, then with pan cover, and bake in 350-degree oven for 15 minutes. Remove cover, add hot wine, cover again and continue baking for 40 minutes, basting occasionally. Remove from oven, place trout on serving dish, strain pan liquid and save.

Blend 2 tablespoons butter with flour, add pan gravy and cream, stirring constantly until gravy thickens. Add ¼ cup butter, a little at a time, beating well until smooth. Pour over trout and serve.

German Trout Pudding

The native German *braun forelle* (brown trout) is traditionally used in this recipe, but you may substitute any firm-fleshed trout.

1½ cups rice
1 small onion, sliced
2 tablespoons olive oil
2 tablespoons tomato sauce
½ teaspoon salt
½ teaspoon pepper
1 egg, slightly beaten
2 tablespoons olive oil
1 clove garlic
2 tablespoons tomato sauce
1½ pounds trout flesh, boned, skinned and chopped
¼ pound mushrooms, sliced
1 cup bread crumbs
1 egg, slightly beaten
2 tablespoons butter

Wash and drain rice. Brown onion in olive oil, add 2 tablespoons tomato sauce, rice, salt, pepper and enough water to cover and cook until rice is almost done, adding a little water if needed. Remove from fire, add beaten egg, and let cool.

Brown garlic in oil and remove garlic. Add 2 tablespoons tomato sauce and diced fish and cook for 2 minutes. Add mushrooms and cook for 3 minutes. Cool. Grease well a 2-quart pudding mold and sprinkle all over the bread crumbs. Line mold with partly cooked rice, leaving a large well in center. Fill the well with fish, cover with additional bread crumbs and dot with butter. Bake in 375-degree oven for 45 minutes. Let cool 5 minutes before turning out on a serving dish. Serves six.

Breezy Brook Bake

6 medium trout fillets
2 tablespoons grated onion
1¼ teaspoons dill weed
1 teaspoon salt
¼ teaspoon pepper
1 tablespoon butter or margarine
¾ cup light cream

As its name indicates, this dish is really a breeze to make. Place fillets in a single layer in a well-greased baking dish, 12 x 8 x 2 inches. Sprinkle fish with onion, dill weed, salt and pepper. Dot with butter. Pour cream over fish. Bake in 350-degree oven for 25 to 30 minutes, or until trout flakes easily when tested with a fork.

Trout River Casserole

1 can cheese soup
1½ cans water
½ green pepper, diced
4 green onions, diced
2 cups trout flesh, boned and skinned
1½ cups instant rice
Salt and pepper
Lemon wedges

Heat a can of cheese soup, and add 1½ cans (use the empty soup can) of water. Add this water a little at a time, and stir until all lumps are gone. Add the diced green pepper and green onions. Heat this mixture over a low fire, stirring continuously until it comes to a boil. Then remove from fire.

Break the trout meat into a casserole dish, and add 1½ cups instant rice, plus salt and pepper to taste. Pour in the cheese soup mixture, and stir gently.

Place casserole in a 350-degree oven and bake for 30 minutes. When it's done, there may be some moisture on top, as the rice may not have absorbed it all. If there is too much moisture for convenient serving, spoon or pour it off. Serve the casserole with lemon wedges on the side.

Southern Trout Cornbread

½ pound trout flesh, boned, skinned and chopped

1 cup sifted flour
1 cup cornmeal
4 teaspoons baking powder
¼ cup sugar
½ teaspoon salt
1 egg, beaten
1 cup milk
¼ cup butter or other fat, melted

Sift together flour, cornmeal, baking powder, sugar, and salt. Combine egg, milk, and butter. Add to dry ingredients and mix just enough to moisten. Stir in trout. Place in a well-greased baking dish, 8 X 8 X 2 inches. Bake in a 425-degree oven for 25 to 30 minutes. Serves six.

Kamloops in Wine

3 pounds of trout steaks
Salt and pepper
1½ cups sherry
2 cloves garlic, chopped
½ cup olive oil
Juice of 2 lemons

Grease a deep baking pan, and put the steaks in it. Sprinkle with salt and pepper. Combine other ingredients, and pour over fish. Bake in a 400-degree oven until tender, about half an hour, but do not overcook. Serve immediately.

Baked Rainbow Florentine

1 pound trout flesh, boned, skinned, and chopped
1 cup cooked, drained spinach
2 tablespoons butter or margarine
¼ teaspoon pepper
¼ teaspoon nutmeg
2 tablespoons chopped onion
1 clove garlic, finely chopped
2 tablespoons butter or margarine, melted
3 tablespoons flour
¼ teaspoon salt
1¼ cups milk
2 tablespoons sherry
¼ cup grated Parmesan cheese
3 hard-boiled eggs, sliced
Watercress

Chop spinach. Season with butter, pepper and nutmeg. Spread seasoned spinach in a well-greased, round baking dish, 8 X 2 inches. Cook onion and garlic in butter until tender. Blend in flour and salt. Add milk gradually and cook until thick, stirring constantly. Add sherry and trout flesh and blend thoroughly. An electric mixer or blender may be used. Place mixture over spinach and sprinkle with cheese. Bake in a 350-degree oven for 20 to 25 minutes. Garnish with egg slices and watercress. Serves six.

Truites Farcies Parisienne

6 small brook trout
Lemon juice
Cognac
Salt
Black pepper, freshly ground
6 fillets of sole
3 tablespoons finely chopped shallots
3 teaspoons butter
3 small egg whites
1 ¼ cups heavy cream
Nutmeg
3 tablespoons finely chopped truffles
Sauce Béarnaise (p. 00).

Wash the trout in lemon juice and water. Remove scales and cut a little off the tail fin. Remove other fins. Slit on both sides of the backbone and remove bone and innards. Wash again in lemon juice and water, and dry. Season inside of each trout with a little cognac, salt and pepper. Put the sole fillets through the fine blade of a meat grinder twice. Place in a metal bowl over a bowl of crushed ice. Sauté shallots in 3 teaspoons butter and add to the sole. Mix in the egg whites. Slowly beat in the heavy cream, season with salt, pepper, and nutmeg to taste and add chopped truffles. Carefully spoon this fish mousse into the trout.

Next, make the pastry dough:

6 cups all-purpose flour
¾ teaspoon salt
12 ounces sweet butter
3 tablespoons butter
3 tablespoons oil
6 egg yolks

1 ½ cups ice water
3 egg yolks beaten with 6 tablespoons milk

Sift the flour and salt into a large bowl. Cut the sweet butter into small pieces and work into the flour until it looks like coarse cornmeal. Make a well in the center and put in it the oil, 6 egg yolks, and ice water. Quickly work up to a firm dough and chill for 30 to 45 minutes.

Roll out the chilled dough ¼ inch thick and on it lay a paper pattern shaped to envelop the fish completely. Cut out 6 dough-cases. Enclose fish in dough and brush the top with the egg-yolk mixture. Roll out remaining dough rather thinner and cut out small fluted crescents to resemble fish scales. Put on fish, and brush again with egg mixture. Bake in a preheated 350-degree oven for 40 to 45 minutes. Serve fish on a platter garnished with watercress; and use a slice of a pimento-stuffed olive as an eye on each pastry-enveloped trout.

Serve Sauce Béarnaise separately. Serves six.

Stuffed Trout Bercy

1 teaspoon minced parsley
1 teaspoon minced shallot
1 teaspoon minced chives
Butter
2 tablespoons flour
1 cup milk
1 tablespoon anchovy paste
½ cup soft bread crumbs
6 trout (about 1 pound each)
Salt and pepper
Lemon wedges
Parsley
Shoestring potatoes

Lightly brown the parsley, shallot, and chives in 2 tablespoons of butter. Sprinkle in the flour and cook, stirring, until the mixture is well blended. Stir in the milk and continue cooking over low heat until you have a thick sauce. Add the anchovy paste and blend. Bring to a boil and stir in the bread crumbs—as much as the mixture will hold without becoming crumbly.

Clean and wash the trout and wipe dry. Stuff them with the mixture and close the opening with skewers. Season with salt and pepper, brush with melted butter, and bake in a 400-degree oven for about 20 minutes, turning and basting the trout frequently with melted butter. When done, arrange the trout on a hot platter and garnish with lemon wedges, parsley, and little heaps of crisp shoe-string potatoes. Pass around a dish of Sauce Bercy, made as follows:

1 tablespoon minced shallot
2 tablespoons butter
½ cup dry white wine
½ cup fish fumet or fish stock
½ cup Sauce Velouté
Finely chopped parsley

Sauté the shallot in 1 tablespoon of the butter until it begins to brown. Add the white wine and fumet, mixed together, and the Sauce Veloute. Bring to a boil and let mixture simmer very slowly for a few minutes, stirring frequently. When ready to serve, add the remaining 1 tablespoon butter and a little chopped parsley. Makes about 1½ cups.
Serves six.

Trout Marguery À La Créole

4 medium trout
½ cup thinly sliced onion
1 clove garlic
1 bay leaf
6 parsley sprigs
6 whole cloves
¼ teaspoon cayenne pepper
Salt and pepper
1 tablespoon butter, cut up
½ cup dry white wine
16 oysters, poached in their juices
½ pound fresh mushrooms, quartered and simmered in butter
    and lemon juice
1 ounce of truffles, diced
4 egg yolks
½ to ¾ cup melted butter
¼ teaspoon Tobasco sauce
1 tablespoon minced parsley
24 cooked shrimp, shelled, warmed in butter

Fillet trout and reserve heads, bones and skin. Simmer these trimmings with the onion, garlic, bay leaf, parsley, cloves, cayenne pepper, 1 teaspoon salt and 1 quart water in an enameled saucepan until liquid has reduced by half. Strain.

Salt and pepper the fillets, lay them in one layer in a lightly buttered shallow baking dish, and dot with the cut up butter. Pour on the fish stock, the wine and enough water to barely cover the trout. Bring almost to a simmer on top of the stove, cover with buttered wax paper, and set in the lower third of a preheated 350-degree oven. Bake for 8 to 10 minutes, or until you can pierce the flesh easily with a fork. Drain the stock into a saucepan. Cover the trout with waxed paper and set aside.

Pour the juices from the oysters, mushrooms and truffles (if canned) into the fish-poaching stock and boil down rapidly until liquid has reduced to 1 cup. Cool slightly. Beat the egg yolks in a bowl until thick and sticky and gradually beat in the liquid. Return to saucepan and stir over low heat until lightly thickened (do not overheat or egg yolks will scramble). Remove from heat and beat in the melted butter slowly, so that the sauce thickens to a cream. Beat in the Tabasco sauce and parsley, and season to taste.

Preheat your broiler to red hot shortly before serving. Garnish the trout fillets with the oysters, shrimp, mushrooms and truffles. Cover the baking dish and heat for a few minutes over a pan of boiling water. Spoon the sauce over the trout and garnishes. Set the dish so that the surface is 1 inch from the hot broiler element for 30 to 40 seconds, until the sauce begins to brown lightly. Serves eight.

Baked Trout Montbarry

6 trout (10 to 12 oz. each), cleaned and washed
Salt
Pepper, freshly ground
1 teaspoon finely chopped parsley
1 teaspoon minced onion
1 tablespoon minced chives
1 teaspoon minced chervil
3 tablespoons finely chopped mushrooms
Fresh tarragon leaves
2 tablespoons melted butter
4 egg yolks
1 ounce brandy
5 tablespoons fresh bread crumbs
5 tablespoons grated Gruyère cheese
Paprika

Season the trout with salt and pepper. Generously butter a baking dish and line with parsley, onion, chives, chervil, mushrooms and tarragon leaves. Put the trout on top and pour on the melted butter. Cover the dish with buttered foil, and bake in a 400-degree oven for 10 to 12 minutes. Beat the egg yolks with the brandy mixture over them, then sprinkle with the bread crumbs mixed with the Gruyère cheese and a little dusting of paprika. Return to the oven and bake until the crumbs are a golden brown. Serve in the baking dish, accompanied by large broiled onions, and thick tomato slices, grilled, with a sautéed mushroom on each slice. Serves six.

Trout St. Petersburg

2 pounds of trout fillets
Salt and pepper
Flour
1 large onion
2 medium-sized carrots
2 stalks celery
2 sliced dill pickles
1 can (6 oz.) tomato paste
1 tablespoon flour
Worcestershire sauce

Skin and slice fillets, season with salt and pepper, roll in flour and fry. Slice onion and carrots and fry in plenty of shortening until well done. Remove carrots and onions to a dish, and in the same fat fry celery. Remove celery to other vegetables and mix with two sliced dill pickles. Put a little more fat in the frying pan, add the tomato paste, and simmer. To this add slowly 1 tablespoon flour, stirring constantly until there are no lumps. Put the vegetables back into this mixture. Season with salt and pepper and a dash of Worcestershire sauce. Add ¼ cup fish stock; if still too thick, add more. Put the trout in a shallow pan, surround with boiled potatoes, pour over it, and bake in a 375-degree oven for 10 to 15 minutes.

Baked Brook Trout Quebecoise

3 ounces fresh butter
1 tablespoon chopped green onions
½ pound of salt pork (cut in fine julienne strips)
6 medium brook trout
12 slices bacon

1 teaspoon lemon juice
¼ teaspoon Worcestershire sauce
Salt and pepper

Clean fish, removing head. Place butter in an open baking pan, add the green onions and salt pork, saute lightly, then place trout, which has been rolled in bacon, into the pan. Bake in a 400-degree oven until browned evenly on both sides. Remove trout to a platter.

Add to the pan the lemon juice, Worcestershire sauce, salt and pepper to taste. Bring to a boil and pour over trout. Serve with lemon wedges and steamed potatoes on a bouquet of fresh parsley.

Romanian Trout Cu Ciapa

2½-3 pounds of trout fillets
Olive oil
Parsley and fennel
3 medium onions, sliced
Paprika
Salt and pepper
2¼ tablespoons flour
3 or 4 medium tomatoes, sliced

Cut the trout into slices of desired thickness and brown in hot, pure olive oil. Pour a little olive oil into a baking dish, sprinkle with chopped parsley and fennel, and place the browned trout on top.

Sauté the onions in 3 tablespoons olive oil or butter. Remove to a saucepan, add paprika, salt and pepper, flour, mixing well. Add tomatoes and cook a little. Add cold water, mix and cook for about 5 minutes longer.

Pour this over the trout stirring constantly and bake until tender in medium heat.

Luxembourg Mint Trout

2 medium trout fillets
½ cup milk
½ cup flour
½ cup bread or cracker crumbs
2 tablespoons melted butter
¼ teaspoon dried mint or 1 teaspoon chopped fresh mint leaves
Salt and pepper

Skin fillets and dip into milk. Roll them in flour, dip them in milk again, and roll them in crumbs. Set the fillets in a greased baking dish and baste them with the melted butter, to which the mint has been added. Season with salt and pepper to taste. Bake in a 425-degree oven for about 10 minutes.

Baked Trout Lisbon

4 medium trout
Salt
Lemon juice
⅓ cup cream
½ cup shredded Parmesan cheese
½ cup fine cracker crumbs
 2 tablespoons finely chopped green onion (or parsley, if you
      prefer)
4 thick tomato slices
Pepper
2 tablespoons butter
¼ cup dry vermouth

Remove heads from trout after washing and cleaning. Sprinkle the inside cavity of each trout with salt and squeeze in a little lemon juice. Dip the trout in cream, then in a mixture of cheese, cracker crumbs and onion. Arrange the trout in a shallow baking pan. Place tomato slice on each trout, and sprinkle with salt and pepper. Dot with butter and add vermouth. Bake in a 375-degree oven until tender, about 40 minutes.

Stuffed Red Trout À La Stockholm

This is the delectable way they prepare it at the Bromma Airport Restaurant:

1 medium trout
Dry oatmeal
Salt and pepper
2 tablespoons butter
2 tablespoons chopped onion
½ cup bread crumbs
1 tablespoon minced parsley
½ clove garlic, mashed
1 teaspoon butter
1 tablespoon boiled onion, cold and chopped
1 tablespoon soft butter
1 egg yolk

Salt and pepper
¼ cup fish stock
¼ cup dry wine

Have trout slit down the back from head to tail and boned. Roll in oatmeal and season with salt and pepper. Put the 2 tablespoons of butter and the chopped onion in a shallow baking dish and place the trout on top of it. Fill the trout with a stuffing made with the bread crumbs, parsley, garlic frizzled in a teaspoon of butter, cold onion, soft butter, egg yolk, and salt and pepper, mixed well. Sew up the opening. Pour the stock and wine over the trout and bake in a 400-degree oven for 15 to 20 minutes, or until trout flakes easily when tested with a fork. Sprinkle chopped parsley over before serving, and serve the broth as a sauce.

5
Broiled Trout

Charcoal-Broiled Trout

Simple charcoal-broiling is one of the easiest ways of preparing trout, and over the years, I've had them charcoal-broiled in many different ways: impaled on sticks and held over the coals, packed in clay, and wrapped in wet newspapers or large leaves. The following two methods, though, I have found to be the most tasty.

METHOD I: Clean and wash trout. Dip them in flour and then in melted butter. Salt and pepper them and arrange them securely in a wire grill. Grill over hot coals for about 4 to 6 minutes, depending upon the size of the fish. Brush with butter while cooking (use a good-sized pastry brush or a small paintbrush). The trout should have a nice crispy coating, but be careful not to overcook them. Serve with potatoes sauted over the outdoor fire or baked under it.

METHOD II: Arrange trout in S-shapes on long skewers, or make rings of the fish by running the skewers through both head and tail. Dip them in flour, then in melted butter, and sprinkle with salt and pepper. Broil them over the coals until just cooked through, brushing with butter during the process. Serve with lemon or lime wedges and melted butter, or with Sauce Hollandaise.

Broiled Trout California

4 small trout
¼ cup lemon juice
½ teaspoon Ac'cent
Few grains pepper
Melted butter or margarine

Clean and wash trout. Rub inside with lemon juice, Ac'cent, salt and pepper.

Place on broiler rack and brush with melted butter. Broil with the surface of the trout 3 to 4 inches below the source of heat for 8 minutes. Turn, brush with melted butter and broil for 5 to 8 minutes longer, until trout flake easily with a fork.

Serve with California Sauce and garnish with lemon wedges and fresh mint.

Trout Kebabs Keuka

This recipe is from my home region of Keuka Lake, in the Finger Lakes of central New York State, where either the lake trout or the magnificent Finger Lakes rainbow trout is used. You may begin with any whole trout.

> 3 pounds firm-fleshed trout
> 12 onions, peeled and quartered
> Juice of 1 lemon
> 2 whole cloves
> 4 bay leaves
> 1 teaspoon rosemary
> 1 cup claret (the New York clarets, such as Taylor New York
>   State, are among the finest)
> ¼ cup salad oil

Start a charcoal fire in your outdoor grill. Next, trim trout and cut into 2-inch chunks. Place trout chunks and onion quarters in a marinade of the other ingredients for about 1 hour prior to cooking. This way, by the time your trout is fully marinated, the charcoal fire will be reduced to a good bed of red-hot coals.

String fish on skewers, alternating with onions. Broil kebabs over coals just until tender and flaky—10 to 15 minutes. Turn twice while broiling, brushing each time with the marinade.

When done, lay skewers on a hot platter, bring to the table with small bundles of dried bay leaves around the edge of the platter, lighted. The smoky fragrance of the bay leaves add immeasurably to the fish flavor. Serve kebabs with the rest of the good claret.

Grilled Trout Honolulu

> 6 medium trout
> 1 cup soy sauce

4 tablespoons brown sugar
¼ cup sherry
1 tablespoon fresh chopped ginger, or 1 teaspoon ground ginger
2 garlic cloves, crushed
½ cup melted butter or margarine
¼ pound almonds, finely ground
1 cup cornmeal
½ teaspoon paprika

Clean and wash trout and lay them in a shallow pan or baking dish. Combine soy sauce, brown sugar, wine, ginger, and garlic. Pour sauce over trout, allowing it to marinate at least 1 hour. Remove fish from sauce, drain on paper towels. Brush both sides of fish with melted butter. Add any remaining butter to sauce. Combine almonds, cornmeal and paprika. Roll fish in this mixture. Grill over red-hot coals for 5 to 8 minutes on each side, brushing with remaining sauce.

Tarragon Butter Lake Trout

½ cup lemon juice
1 tablespoon dried tarragon leaves
¼ teaspoon salt
¼ teaspoon pepper
4 large trout steaks
Butter

In a shallow dish, combine lemon juice, tarragon, salt and pepper.
Wash trout steaks and dry with paper towels. Place in marinade, turning to coat both sides. Cover and refrigerate for about 1½ hours, turning steaks once or twice.
Remove steaks from marinade, and arrange on rack in broiler pan. Reserve marinade. Top each steak with a thin pat of butter. Broil, 4 inches from heat, for 5 minutes. Turn steaks, brush with marinade, and top each with another thin pat of butter. Broil 5 to 8 minutes longer, or until fish flakes easily with a fork.

Sesame Rainbow Trout

6 medium rainbow trout
Salt and pepper
½ cup cooking oil
¼ cup sesame seeds, toasted

¼ cup lemon juice
1 teaspoon salt
¼ teaspoon pepper
3 lemons

Clean and wash trout. Sprinkle inside with a little salt and pepper. Combine oil, sesame seeds, lemon juice, 1 teaspoon salt and ¼ teaspoon pepper, mixing well. To grill, place fish in well-greased hinged wire basket. Brush fish inside and out with sauce and close basket. Cook over medium-hot coals for 5 to 8 minutes. Brush again with sauce. Turn, and cook 5 to 8 minutes more, or until fish flakes easily when tested with a fork. Serve with hot lemon wedges, prepared thus:

Cut thin slice off top and bottom of lemon. Using sharp knife, cut lemon into 6 wedges, cutting to but not through the lemon base. Sprinkle inside of lemon with paprika. Place stuffed green olive in center, if desired. Heat on grill with fish.

Mormon Broiled Trout

This early Mormon method of preparing trout results in a very mild-tasting fish. Serve it with just bread and butter for a very simple but delicious meal.

2 tablespoons melted butter
4 small trout
Sage leaves, finely crushed
Salt and pepper

In a cake pan of suitable girth and height, put ¼ inch of water. Sprinkle the melted butter on top of the water, and place your trout in the pan. Sprinkle the trout lightly with sage, and salt and pepper to taste. Broil in a 450-degree oven for 6 minutes. Turn trout over, sprinkle the other side in the same fashion and broil for another 6 minutes.

6
Poached Trout

Poached Whole Trout

First, make this white wine court bouillon:

1 quart water
1 quart dry white wine
3 carrots
3 white onions
9 broken peppercorns
1 clove
1 large bay leaf
3 celery tops (with leaves)
2 sprigs parsley
1 sprig thyme
1 tablespoon salt

Simmer the other ingredients in the wine and water for 35 minutes. Strain the resulting broth and cool.

Next, carefully wrap your cleaned and wash trout in cheesecloth or thin cotton, leaving a length of material protruding on either end to use as handles. The cloth prevents the fish from breaking up and makes it easier to serve. Place the wrapped fish on its side in a poaching pan. Pour in the court bouillon (it should come nearly halfway up on the fish).

Poach, allowing approximately 7 minutes per pound of fish. When properly cooked, the fish should be intact, but it should flake easily. Serve with hot melted butter.

Truite Au Bleu

This French recipe is one of the most magnificent and delicious ways of cooking trout there is. However, the trout must be alive immediately prior to preparing. The reason for this is that the color comes from the lubricant which makes the fish slippery. When the trout is alive, this film is what keeps him waterproof—without it, he would drown. If this film has dried or been wiped off, then the trout is no good for this recipe.

First, brew this hearty white wine court bouillon in your poacher:

    1 quart water
    1 quart white wine
    2 stalks celery (with leaves)
    1 large onion, quartered
    2 whole carrots
    Few lettuce leaves
    2 bay leaves
    Handful of parsley
    1 teaspoon dill weed
    8 whole peppercorns
    1 tablespoon salt

If you like, you may add 1 to 2 pounds of fish heads and bones. Allow to bubble for about an hour. In the meantime, dilute some tarragon vinegar in a large kettle at the ratio of ⅔ vinegar to ⅓ water to cover trout. Bring to boil.

When bouillon is ready, strain it and keep it bubbling while you blue the trout.

An instant before blueing, kill the fish with a sharp blow on the back of the head and clean them, taking care to handle them as little as possible. Leave the fins on the fish and do not scrape, or even wash them, in order to preserve the film. With large kitchen tongs, grasp each fish by the lower jaw and dip it in the kettle of hot vinegar water. The vinegar in the water turns the skin of the trout a vivid metallic blue.

When properly blue, place it in the poacher. The court bouillon will cease bubbling for a few minutes, but when it becomes active again, turn the heat low so that it barely simmers. Depending on their size, the fish should be ready in 15 to 20 minutes. Test with a fork, then raise the poacher rack carefully, allowing liquid to drip off.

Remove the eyes and serve with quartered lemon, parsley, boiled potatoes and melted butter, or arrange on a platter with a saddle of Sauce Hollandaise over each fish. A pink or white wine such as Almaden Grenache Rose or Pinot Blanc is the mate to such rich fare.

This was originally an outdoor method, and the trout were cooked as soon as they were caught. Many restaurants have tanks of live trout so that they can pull them out, give them a smack, and pop them into the cauldron on order. *C'est magnifique!*

Trout Poached In Beer

1 can of beer
1 carrot, sliced
1 onion, sliced
1 stalk celery, sliced
8 peppercorns
5 whole cloves
1 dime-size piece of bay leaf
4 large trout fillets

Pour beer into 10-inch skillet, let it come to a boil, add vegetables and spices, and simmer for 10 minutes. Arrange fillets in stock and simmer for 10 to 15 minutes, according to thickness of fish. When fish is poached, transfer to baking dish and prepare sauce:

2 tablespoons butter
2 tablespoons flour
Salt and white pepper
2 egg yolks
¼ cup light cream or milk
¼ cup grated Parmesan cheese
½ cup grated Gruyere cheese
2 tablespoons fresh parsley, chopped

Reduce juices in pan to 1 cup and strain. In small pan melt butter and remove from fire. Add flour, mix, and then add salt and pepper, egg yolks and milk. Stir until smooth, put back on fire and blend in cheeses. When cheese is well blended, add fish stock and cook, while stirring, until smooth. Pour sauce over fish and broil until golden brown. Sprinkle with fresh chopped parsley and serve with either beer or a good sturdy ale.

Trout À La Newburg

First, prepare this court bouillon:

1½ cups boiling water
½ cup dry white wine

¼ teaspoon salt
2 slices of garlic
2 small onions
1 bay leaf
6 peppercorns
⅛ teaspoon thyme
6 slices carrot
3 sprigs parsley

Cook together for 30 minutes at simmering temperature. Meanwhile, prepare the following:

1 pound trout flesh, boned and skinned
1 tablespoon brandy
¼ cup sherry
2 tablespoons butter
1 cup evaporated milk (undiluted)
1 teaspoon lemon juice
3 egg yolks
¼ teaspoon cayenne
Salt

Cut the trout into small cubes.

When bouillon is done, poach trout in it for 5 minutes. When poached, put the fish, butter, wine, brandy, salt and cayenne in a double boiler and heat smoking hot. Beat the yolks and combine with the evaporated milk (sour cream may be substituted for the milk and lemon juice). Cook with the hot fish for 1 minute. Remove from fire and add the lemon juice. Serve on very hot plates.

New Hampshire Boiled Trout

1 trout of 4 pounds, or 2 trout of 2 pounds each
3 stalks celery, sliced
1 teaspoon monosodium glutamate
Juice of 1 lemon
½ cup dry wine
1 medium onion, sliced
2 medium carrots, thinly sliced
1 bay leaf
1 quart water
Rind of ¼ lemon
3 medium potatoes
Salt and pepper

Combine all ingredients but the fish and potatoes and cook slowly for 30 minutes. Meanwhile, clean and wash trout.

Add trout and potatoes, cover, and cook for 35 to 40 minutes.

Serve trout with small portion of the juice or with lemon butter (simply heat the amount of butter desired and add lemon juice to taste) and parsley.

The remaining liquid can be used for soup.

Wisconsin Milk-Boiled Trout

1 trout of 4 pounds, or 2 trout of 2 pounds each
3 stalks celery, sliced
½ medium onion, sliced
1 bay leaf
Pinch of thyme
Salt and pepper
Parsley, finely chopped

Boil trout in milk and other ingredients for 30 to 35 minutes. Boiling the fish in milk preserves the flavor. Serve trout topped with lemon butter (simply heat the amount of butter desired and add lemon juice to taste) and sprinkle with finely chopped parsley.

Trout Antoinette

This famous recipe was a great favorite of Marie Antoinette, and makes a very firm-fleshed trout with no fish odor.

2 quarts water
6 bay leaves
½ cup vinegar
1 teaspoon salt
9 peppercorns, or 1 teaspoon black pepper
2 medium trout
3 heaping tablespoons butter
⅛ teaspoon paprika
⅛ teaspoon ground allspice

Put water in a pot, add bay leaves, vinegar, salt, and peppercorns (or black pepper), and bring to a boil. Boil trout for about 7 minutes. Remove from bouillon, drain, remove skin, and place on plate.

Melt butter in frying pan, add paprika and allspice. Pour hot over trout.

Trout With Vermouth

2 cups dry vermouth
½ teaspoon salt
8 trout (8 to 10 oz. each)
8 egg yolks
10 ounces butter (2½ sticks), cut into small pieces
2 tablespoons light cream

Heat the vermouth with the salt, add the trout and poach for about 10 minutes, or until done. Remove to a heated fire-proof serving dish and keep hot. Reduce the cooking liquid quickly until it becomes thick. Put in the top of a double boiler over hot, not boiling, water. Add the egg yolks, butter, and cream, and beat well with a French wire whip until the butter melts and the sauce thickens. Do not let the water boil. Correct the seasoning, if necessary, and pour over the trout. Place under the broiler for a minute or two to brown the top. Serves four.

7
Cold Trout

Lake Tahoe Trout Cocktail

1 16-inch trout, or 3 8-inch trout
Water
1 teaspoon salt
½ teaspoon pepper
3 crushed bay leaves
¼ teaspoon Worcestershire sauce
¼ teaspoon thyme
Cocktail sauce

Clean and wash trout, removing heads and tails. Cut the fish into pieces 3 or 4 inches long, and put into a stew kettle. Add enough water to cover. Add salt, pepper, bay leaves, Worcestershire sauce and thyme.

Heat to a boil, and let boil for about 10 minutes. Remove kettle from fire, and let fish and water cool so that the flavor of the broth is absorbed into the meat. When cool, the fish pieces should be removed and the meat flaked from bones and skin.

Place the shredded trout in cocktail glasses (you should get 4 or 5 servings from the amount of fish specified), and place in refrigerator to chill. Just before you bring the glasses to the table, cover the meat with cocktail sauce. Serve with lemon slices.

Viennese Pickled Trout

12 small trout
1 bottle white wine
6 peppercorns
1 carrot, thinly sliced
4 small white onions
2 cloves

1 bay leaf
1 teaspoon tarragon leaves
Pinch of thyme
1 teaspoon salt
1 teaspoon freshly ground pepper
¼ cup wine vinegar
½ cup olive oil
12 thin slices of lemon
1 medium onion, thinly sliced

Clean and wash the trout. Prepare a court bouillon with the wine, peppercorns, carrot, small onions (stick 2 cloves in each), bay leaf, tarragon, thyme, salt, pepper and vinegar. Bring to a boil and let it boil for 15 minutes. Add the trout and poach about 5 minutes, or until they are just cooked through. Remove the fish to a serving dish.

Add the olive oil, lemon slices and sliced onion to the broth. Reduce it to 1 cup and when cool, pour it over the trout. Chill for 24 hours before serving.

These may be made with their own marinade for the sauce, or with mayonnaise. A salad of cucumbers, tomatoes stuffed with cucumbers, or Salade Russe are good additions.

Cold Trout In Jelly

6 medium poached whole trout
White and shell of 1 egg
1½ envelopes gelatin
Green onion, leek, chives, tarragon leaves
Hard-boiled eggs

After poaching the trout, remove them to a platter and chill. Reduce the bouillon to 3 cups and clarify with the lightly beaten egg white and shells. Strain. Soak the gelatin in ⅓ cup of water and combine it with the boiling broth. Chill until it is thick and syrupy.

The fish may be decorated as elaborately as you wish. Or you may prefer to serve them plain, simply masked with the jelly. If you want a spectacular dish, remove about half of the skin from the chilled, poached trout. Then use the green stems of onions, leeks, chives, green tarragon leaves, and hard-boiled egg to make flowers on the flesh.

Pour enough of the jelly over the decorated, or plain, trout to mask it thoroughly. Put the platter with the fish and a bowl of the rest of the jelly in the refrigerator to chill. Just before serving, chop the rest of the jelly very fine and garnish the fish platter with it. Serve with Mayonaise Sauce or Sauce Remoulade.

VARIATION: Reduce the broth to 1 cup and add 1 cup red wine or port wine. Add 1 envelope of gelatin to make the jelly.

Cold Trout With Dill Sauce

8 medium poached whole trout (Chapter 6)
Finely chopped dill, parsley and chives
Sliced hard-boiled eggs
Sliced cucumber

After poaching the trout until they are just cooked through, remove them to a platter and chill thoroughly. When chilled, remove part of the skin from the top of the trout, leaving the heads and tails intact. Sprinkle with finely chopped dill, parsley and chives. Arrange alternate slices of cucumber and hard-boiled egg on each trout.

Serve with Sour Cream Sauce:

1½ cups sour cream
1 tablespoon fresh dill
1 teaspoon grated onion
1 teaspoon dry mustard
½ cup finely chopped hard-boiled egg
Salt and pepper

Combine all ingredients well, seasoning to taste with the salt and pepper, and pour over trout. Garnish with whole parsley.

Danish Jellied Trout With Dill And Lemon

1 cup dry white wine
1 tablespoon salt
1 small onion, sliced
6 sprigs fresh dill
4 cups water
6 small trout
4 cups aspic
Sliced truffles

Combine wine, salt, onion, dill, and water in fish cooker or deep kettle. Bring to a simmer. Place the trout in liquid, preferable on a rack. Bring back to simmering, and simmer gently for 5 minutes. Carefully remove the trout. Make diagonal slits in the skin of each trout just below the head and above the tail and remove the skin carefully. Leave heads and tails intact. Place the trout on a serving platter (traditionally a silver one) in orderly rows. Chill. Spoon chilled but still liquid aspic over trout. Make as many layers as desired, chilling after each layer is applied. Decorate trout with sliced truffles and cover with another layer of aspic. Decorate platter with additional chopped aspic, inner leaves of Boston lettuce, lemon twists, and dill sprigs. Serve with Mustard Sauce.

Swedish Jellied Trout In Tomato Juice

1   pound trout
1   package gelatin
1   bouillon cube
1   teaspoon salt
6   allspice
2   bay leaves
1½ cups tomato juice

Boil trout in 2 cups water, salt, and spices until well done. Cool and pick out bones and skin. Flake fish and place in mold (preferably a fish shaped one). Strain broth and add tomato juice and bouillon cube and bring to a boil. Add gelatin to hot broth and pour over trout in mold. When set and chilled, turn out on a platter and garnish with parsley, and serve with mayonnaise. Serves six.

8
Deep-Fried Trout

French-Fried Trout

12 small trout
2 eggs
2 cups bread crumbs
4 tablespoons butter
3 tablespoons olive oil
Flour
Salt and pepper
Fat for frying

Clean and wash the trout. Beat the eggs lightly, and crush or roll the crumbs. Dust the trout with flour, sprinkle with salt and pepper, dip in the egg, and then in the crumbs. Cook the trout in deep hot fat heated to 370 degrees, until the fish brown and get crisp on the outside. Serve with Sauce Tartare or Sauce Remoulade.

Deep-Fried Trout Cutlets

1 pound of trout flesh, boned and flaked
2 cups creamy mashed potatoes
1 tablespoon grated onion
1½ teaspoons salt
1 teaspoon paprika
Flour
1 egg
Bread crumbs
Fat for frying

Mash trout flesh. Combine it with the potatoes and seasonings and form into cutlets. Roll the cutlets in flour, dip in beaten egg and roll in crumbs. Chill for one hour. Fry in deep fat heated to 390 degrees. Serve with Sauce Hollandaise.

Roze Trout Croquettes

A Parisian chef named Roze invented the menu in the late eighteenth century, and these croquettes of his are one of the world's great recipes.

1 pound of trout fillets, skin intact
1/3 loaf day-old bread
1 small onion (about 1½ inches in diameter)
1 egg
1 teaspoon mustard
1 tablespoon soft butter
⅛ teaspoon nutmeg
Salt and pepper
2 egg whites
Cracker crumbs
Beef grease

Place the fillets in a pot and cover them with just enough water in which to boil them. When thoroughly cooked, skin the fillets and mash the flesh with a fork. Crumble the day-old bread well. Chop onion, mix with bread crumbs, then mix both with trout flesh in a mixing bowl. Add the egg, mustard, soft butter, nutmeg, and salt and pepper to taste, mixing well. After thoroughly mixing all these ingredients, form into round balls about 1½ inches in diameter.

Beat the two egg whites stiff. Roll the balls into the egg whites, then into cracker crumbs.

Fry croquettes in a French fryer in 400-degree beef fat until they are almost browned (about 7 minutes). Remove from grease and let drain about 3 minutes (to allow grease to reheat). Put croquettes back in grease until they are slightly browned, shaking them a little as they brown. Drain.

Serve with Sauce Tartare, Mayonnaise Sauce, or Sauce Verte.

Part II
Salmon

Salmon enjoys a richly deserved international reputation as a gourmet food. Like beef, it is also popular with people of both plain and fancy taste, and it is eaten even by some members of that small group who dislike fish in general. Both fresh and quick-frozen salmon are readily obtainable. Smoked, salted, potted, kippered, and canned salmon may be purchased nearly everywhere.

Most of the salmon eaten in the United States now comes from Alaska, Puget Sound, and the Columbia River. There once was a time when salmon was also plentiful along the Eastern seaboard, but over the years the rivers were fished so ruthlessly and relentlessly that the eastern catch is no longer of commercial significance. Nearly all Eastern salmon offered in the markets comes from Canada's Atlantic seaboard. In New York especially, smoked Nova Scotia salmon is sold as an expensive delicacy.

The decline of salmon fishing in the East served as an example for the West Coast. To prevent its own demise, the Far Western salmon industry has worked diligently with the government in efforts to perpetuate the great "runs" of salmon that appear each year in Western rivers. The migrations are not as large as they were once, but they still are magnificent spectacles.

Like trout, there are several different varieties of salmon. Some live in salt water and come into fresh water only to spawn, and others, called landlocked salmon, live their entire lives in fresh water.

Any sportsman who goes fishing for salmon on the Pacific coast will find unrivaled accommodations there for handling his catch. He can have it packed in ice, frozen stiff, smoked, or even canned with his own name on the label.

The salmon of the north Pacific is basically a salt-water fish. It spends most of its life in the open sea, then returns unerringly to the fresh-water stream where it was born. There it spawns and usually dies. Its off-spring migrate back to the sea, to renew the mysterious and fascinating cycle.

The mature salmon is a magnificent fish ranging in size from six to sixty pounds, or larger. It is a vigorous game fish, which leaps seemingly insurmountable crashing rapids during the final journey to its spawning grounds, often as far as 200 miles inland.

Salmon flesh varies in color from pale pink to red. Eastern salmon is usually more pale than the westerners, and often less firm.

In the interior of Alaska, I have visited Indian fishing camps where salmon catching provides the only income during the summer. I say "catching" instead of fishing because they use fish wheels. The fish wheel is an ingenious mechanism which is believed to have been introduced from the Orient in the late eighteenth century. It resembles a small mill water wheel built of light poles lashed together with thongs, and turned by the current. At each set of spokes, a slanting trough scoops up the massed salmon rushing upstream and slides them down into a box on the side of the wheel. The native has then only to paddle out and pick up his catch.

From time immemorial, Athabascan families have been coming down to the rivers in summer to catch salmon and dry it, and the Indians are the only people allowed to use fish wheels. The salmon are split and cleaned and hung out on poles in the sun. The best parts are further cured by smoking. The sourdoughs call it "squaw candy." The fish for the sled dogs is merely dried to a leathery consistency and then packed away in bags for the winter.

One of the most mouth-watering aromas I have ever encountered was on an August day when I stepped into a tall birch-bark smokehouse on the bank of the Tanana River, where strips of dried pink salmon hung on racks clear to the ceiling.

Salmon fishing is also tremendously popular in Scandanavia, the British Isles, and even in places like Argentina, where landlocked salmon reach magnificent proportions.

9

Sautéed Salmon

Salmon Sautéed Streamside

The simplest way to prepare your salmon steaks is to sauté them in a mixture of butter and a small amount of oil. An oily fish, the salmon does not require much additional lubrication. Flour steaks lightly, brown on one side and turn carefully. Salt and pepper and continue cooking until the flesh flakes easily when tested with a fork. Do not overcook. Pour the pan juices over the steaks, if you like. It is rich, oily and flavorful, and needs no sauce, but serve it with lemon if you have it.

Alaskan Sockeye Cream Sauté

4 salmon steaks
Flour
4 tablespoons butter
Salt and pepper
1/3 cup sherry
1 cup heavy cream
Beurre manière
Chopped parsley

Dust the steaks lightly with flour and saute them in butter until nicely browned on both sides. Salt and pepper to taste. When the salmon is done, remove it to a hot platter. Add the sherry to the pan and let it cook down for a minute or two. Prepare beurre manière by kneading 2 tablespoons of butter with 3 tablespoons of flour. Add cream and beurre manière to pan and stir until nicely thickened. Add chopped parsley, taste for seasoning, and pour over the salmon.

Hudson Bay Salmon Sauté

½ pound mushrooms
8 tablespoons butter

71

Salt and pepper
2 cups Sauce Velouté
4 salmon steaks
Flour
8 anchovy fillets
1 lemon, sliced

Chop mushrooms very fine and sauté them in 4 tablespoons of butter until they are thoroughly cooked and almost a puree. Salt and pepper to taste and combine with the Sauce Velouté. Dust the salmon steaks with flour and saute in the remaining butter until they are nicely browned and flake easily when tested with a fork. Serve with the sauce poured around the fish. Garnish with anchovy fillets and slices of lemon.

Queen Charlotte Salmon Sauté

½ cup finely chopped onion
6 tablespoons butter
4 salmon steaks or fillets
Flour
1 clove garlic
1 teaspoon tarragon
Lemon juice

Sauté the chopped onions in 2 tablespoons of butter until just soft. Remove from the pan and add the remaining butter to the pan. Dust the salmon with the flour mixed with about 2 teaspoons of the curry powder. Season with salt, pepper. Sauté the steaks very quickly just until they flake when tested with a fork. Remove to a hot platter. Return the onions to the pan and reheat. Add the rest of the curry powder and blend well. Gradually stir in the sour cream and heat but do not boil. Check seasoning. Pour sauce over the salmon and serve with rice.

Salmon Piquante

1 clove garlic, finely chopped
1 small onion, finely chopped
5 tablespoons butter
4 salmon steaks
Flour
2 tablespoons lemon juice
3 tablespoons Worcestershire sauce

½ cup tomato sauce
1 garlic dill pickle, chopped
Salt and pepper

Sauté the garlic and onion in butter until just soft. Dust the fish with flour and add to the pan. Cook until they are nicely browned and just cooked through. Add the lemon juice, the Worcestershire sauce and the tomato sauce to the pan and let it cook down for a minute. Remove the salmon to a hot platter. Add the pickle to the sauce and taste for seasoning—it may need a little more Worcestershire sauce. Pour the sauce over the steaks and serve.

Iverness-Style Salmon Sauté

1 tablespoon paprika
Flour
Salt
4 salmon steaks
6 tablespoons butter
½ cup white wine
1½ cups sour cream

Mix a little paprika with the flour and dip the salmon steaks in the mixture. Sauté them quickly in butter until the fish flakes easily. Season with salt. Remove the steaks to a hot platter. Add the wine to the pan, stir it around to mix well, and let it cook down to ¼ cup. Add the sour cream and additional paprika, blending it well, and heat through but do not let it boil. Taste for seasoning and pour over the salmon steaks. Serve with rice.

Siskayou Salmon Burgers

2 cups salmon flesh, boned, skinned and flaked
1 medium onion, chopped
2 tablespoons butter or margarine
1/3 cup dry bread crumbs
2 beaten eggs
¼ cup snipped parsley
1 teaspoon dry mustard
1/3 cup dry bread crumbs

Cook onion in butter or margarine until tender. Add 1/3 cup crumbs, eggs, parsley, mustard, and salmon. Mix well. Shape into 6 patties and roll in remaining bread crumbs. In heavy skillet, melt about 3 tablespoons shortening. Cook patties over medium heat until brown on one side. Carefully turn and brown on other side, melting a slice of cheese on top if you wish. Serve on toasted buns. Serves six.

Sebago Lake Salmon Patties

1½ cups salmon flesh, boned, skinned and flaked
½ teaspoon salt
1 egg
1½ cups mashed potatoes
1 tablespoon minced onion
⅛ teaspoon pepper
Flour
Cooking oil

Combine all ingredients except flour and oil. Shape mixture into patties and roll in flour. Brown in oil.
Serve with Lemon Cheese Sauce:

2 tablespoons butter or margarine
2 tablespoons all-purpose flour
½ teaspoon salt
⅛ teaspoon pepper
1 cup milk
2 egg yolks, beaten
½ cup shredded sharp process American cheese
2 tablespoons lemon juice

Melt butter, blend in flour, salt and pepper. Add milk all at once. Cook and stir until thickened. Stir in egg yolks, cheese and lemon juice. Pour over salmon patties. Serves six.

Yukon Treasure Cakes

2 eggs, beaten
5 slices day-old bread, shredded
2 tablespoons instant minced onion
2 tablespoons parsley flakes
1 tablespoon lemon juice
1 pound salmon flesh, boned, skinned and flaked
¼ pound cheddar cheese
1 tablespoon shortening

Mix eggs, bread, onion, parsley, lemon juice and salmon. Mix well and shape mixture around squares of cheese. Brown on both sides in hot shortening. Serves six.

Chinese Salmon Cakes

1 pound salmon flesh, boned and skinned
1 lemon
2 ounces parsley
2 eggs
1 tablespoon flour
½ cup water
Salt and pepper

Chop salmon and parsley up into very fine pieces or pass them through a mincer. Add flour and eggs. Mix in water, salt and pepper and at last the lemon juice. Shape into small cakes and fry in a hot pan on both sides.

Greek Salmon Omelette

6½ ounces (1 small can) salmon flesh, boned and skinned
4 eggs, separated
4 tablespoons olive oil
1 tablespoon parsley, finely chopped
Salt and pepper

Chop salmon very finely. Beat egg yolks lightly, add 2 tablespoons olive oil and the parsley and season to taste. Pour in a small saucepan and stir over gentle heat until all the ingredients are well blended, but do not allow the mixture to boil. Remove from the heat and mix in the salmon. When the mixture is cold, fold in the stiffly beaten egg whites. Heat the rest of the oil in an omelette pan, pour in the eggs and cook as you would a plain omelette.

10

Baked Salmon

Baked Whole Salmon With Herbs

1 whole salmon, 6 to 8 pounds
¾ cup dry white wine
Pinch of thyme
1 tablespoon fresh basil leaves
3 sprigs fresh tarragon
5 or 6 celery leaves
2 scallions, chopped
2 slices of lemon with peel

Preheat oven to 375 degrees. Clean salmon, leaving whole or removing head. Rinse the fish under cold running water, and place on paper towels to dry. Combine the wine and the rest of the ingredients in a saucepan and heat only enough to warm the wine. Take the pan off the flame, and let the herbs steep in the wine for about a half-hour. Take a double fold of heavy-duty aluminum foil which is a little longer than the fish. Turn the edges of this double sheet up to form a shallow foil pan. Put the fish on another sheet of heavy foil—also double the length of the fish—and bring the edges of the foil across the fish to meet at the middle. Pour the wine mixture over the fish, sprinkle with salt and pepper, and completely encase the fish in foil by crimping the edges together tightly. Put the fish in the foil pan, and place in the oven. Bake 12 to 15 minutes per pound. Test by opening the foil package and seeing if the fish flakes easily when pierced with a fork. Take the fish out of the foil package when done.

Use the pan juices to make the following wine sauce:

¼ pound butter or margarine
2 scallions, finely chopped

6 tablespoons flour
Pan juices
1 cup dry white wine
1 cup boiling water
½ cup heavy cream
Salt and pepper
2 egg yolks

Melt the butter and add scallions. Saute until scallions are limp, but not browned. Stir in flour, using wire whisk to make sure it blends well. Cook over low heat for 3 minutes. Add pan juices, and heat over moderate flame, stirring constantly. Add the white wine and the boiling water, still stirring, and cook until sauce is thickened. Add the cream. Lower heat and don't let the sauce boil again. Taste and correct seasoning. Cool, and process for a few seconds in a blender, so that the sauce is absolutely smooth, or else strain the sauce through a sieve. Just before serving, put the sauce back on the fire, and reheat. Beat the egg yolks lightly, beat in a little of the hot sauce, then beat the yolks into the pan. Cook 2 minutes over low heat, stirring constantly, but do not boil. Pour the sauce over salmon and serve immediately. Serves ten.

King Salmon Bake

Make the stuffing first:

2 onions
1 clove garlic
Butter
1 green pepper, seeded and chopped
4 ripe tomatoes, peeled, seeded and chopped
Chopped parsley
Salt and pepper

Sauté the onions and garlic in butter until just soft. Add green pepper, tomato, parsley, and salt and pepper to taste.

Now prepare fish:

1 Salmon, 4 to 6 pounds
Salt
4 tablespoons vegetable oil

Clean and wash salmon, rubbing inside and out sparingly with salt. Stuff with the sauted vegetables, and use small metal skewers through the edges to secure the salmon and lace with light twine. Place the fish in a lightly oiled pan and oil the surface of the skin. Bake in a 350-degree oven, allowing about 10 minutes per pound, or until the flesh flakes easily from the bone when tested with a fork.

A tomato sauce made with red wine goes best with this, so try the Barbecue Sauce.

Russian River Stuffed Salmon

Make the stuffing first:

2 to 3 cups dry bread crumbs or zweiback crumbs
1 cup ground cooked ham
½ cup finely chopped onion
4 tablespoons butter
2 tablespoons olive oil
¼ cup chopped parsley
1 teaspoon dried or 1 tablespoon fresh tarragon
Salt and pepper

Combine crumbs and ham. Saute the onions in butter and oil until soft, add the other ingredients, and blend thoroughly. If the stuffing is too dry, add 1/3 cup of sherry or vermouth.

Now prepare fish:

1 salmon, 4 to 6 pounds
Salt
4 tablespoons oil
4 strips salt pork

Clean and wash salmon, rubbing inside and out sparingly with salt. Stuff it rather loosely, and either sew up sides, or run skewers through and lace with twine. Place the stuffed fish on a lightly oiled pan and top with salt pork slices. Bake in a 350-degree oven for 40 to 50 minutes, or until the fish flakes easily when tested with a fork. Serve plain or with Sauce Hollandaise.

Klamath Falls Salmon Bake

1 salmon, 4 to 6 pounds
Salt
Lemon

2 green peppers, seeded and cut into fine strips
2 large onions, thinly sliced
3 to 6 sprigs parsley
Salt and pepper
4 tablespoons olive oil
4 strips salt pork
2 cups tomatoes (cooked or canned)

Clean and wash salmon, and rub it with salt and lemon. Stuff it with the green peppers, onions, tomatoes and parsley. Salt and pepper lightly. Place the fish in a lightly oiled baking pan and top with slices of salt pork. Surround it with cooked (or canned) tomatoes and bake in a 350-degree oven for 40 to 60 minutes, basting occasionally with the pan juices. Remove the fish to a hot platter, blend the pan juices and taste for seasoning. Serve the sauce separately. Plain boiled potatoes and French peas are excellent accompaniment.

NOTE: If you like, you can add chopped garlic and red wine to the cooked tomatoes to make a more flavorful sauce.

Baked Salmon Scandinavian

1 salmon, 6 to 8 pounds
1½ pounds whitefish, sole or haddock flesh
3 eggs
1 cup cream
1 teaspoon salt
1 tablespoon chopped fresh dill
½ cup crumbs
4 tablespoons olive oil
4 slices salt pork
Sauce Velouté seasoned with chopped fresh dill and parsley

Put whitefish through the fine blade of a grinder twice. Pound it into a mortar or work it over with a wooden spoon, mixing in the eggs and cream until the whole mixture is well blended and smooth. Work in the salt, the fresh dill and crumbs. Clean and wash salmon and stuff it with mixture. Either sew it up or secure it with skewers and twine. Place the fish on an oiled baking pan and top with salt pork strips. Bake in a 350-degree oven for 1 hour, or until the fish flakes easily when tested with a fork. Serve with Sauce Velouté seasoned with chopped fresh dill and parsley.

Argentine-Style Salmon Steaks

2 salmon steaks
1 teaspoon salt
2 cups sour cream
1 onion, finely chopped
1 tablespoon lemon juice
1 tablespoon chopped fresh dill or tarragon, or 1 teaspoon
        dried tarragon
Parsley

Arrange the steaks in a baking dish and salt lightly. Mix all the other ingredients except the parsley with the sour cream and pour it over the fish. Bake in a 350-degree oven for 35 minutes. Sprinkle with chopped parsley and serve with crisp shoestring potatoes.

Sitka Salmon Steaks

2 salmon steaks
Oil
½ pound mushrooms, sliced
4 tablespoons butter
½ pound shrimp, finely chopped
Salt and pepper
Fennel or tarragon
1 teaspoon salt
1 pint sour cream

Brush the salmon well with oil and place one steak on the bottom of a baking dish. Sauté the mushrooms in butter until just soft, add the chopped shrimp and let it cook for 1 minute. Spread this mixture on the steak in the pan, salt and pepper to taste and top with the second steak. Mix the herbs and 1 teaspoon of salt with the sour cream and pour it over the fish. Bake in a 350-degree oven for 45 minutes or until the fish is done.

Rogue River Salmon Cutlets

2 cups Thick White Sauce
2 teaspoons Worcestershire sauce
2 teaspoons lemon juice
1 tablespoon minced onion
⅛ teaspoon celery salt
2 cups salmon flesh, boned, skinned and flaked

Prepare 2 cups Thick White Sauce. Add Worcestershire sauce, lemon juice, minced onion, and celery salt, and mix well. Add fish to sauce (soft bones can be left in fish, if desired), and chill well.

Form into cutlets and roll in finely sifted dry bread crumbs. Place on greased pan. Bake in 400-degree oven for 20 minutes. Serve with lemon sections and Sauce Tartare.

Cape Breton Salmon Croquettes

1½ cups water
⅔ cup farina
¾ teaspoon salt
1 cup salmon flesh, boned, skinned and flaked
1 teaspoon lemon juice
1 tablespoon finely chopped parsley
Dash of Tabasco sauce
4 teaspoons grated onion
⅛ teaspoon pepper
1 beaten egg
1 cup crushed corn flakes

Bring water to boil. Add farina and salt, stir until thickened. Cook for 5 minutes. Add salmon with lemon juice, parsley, Tabasco, onion and pepper. Form into 8 cylinders. Dip croquettes in egg and coat with corn flake crumbs.

Bake in 350-degree oven for 20 minutes. Serve with sauce made by adding 2 sliced hard-boiled eggs to 1½ cups Medium White Sauce. Serves four.

Trinity River Salmon Bake

1 small dressed salmon, or 6 pound salmon shoulder
¼ cup melted butter
¼ cup minced celery
¼ cup minced onion
½ pound mushrooms, sliced
2 tablespoons minced parsley
2 cups cracker crumbs
½ teaspoon salt
Pepper
¼ teaspoon dried basil

Clean and wash salmon and drain well. Combine the other ingredients into a stuffing, and either fill cavity of whole fish, or, if you are using salmon shoulders, lace them together on two sides first, stuff, then skewer or tie shut. Put the fish in a greased baking dish. Brush with melted butter, and bake uncovered in 350-degree oven for about 18 minutes per pound, or until fish flakes easily but is still moist. Don't let it get overdone and dried out. Serve garnished with lemon slices and chopped parsley.

Atlantic Salmon Casserole

2 pounds salmon flesh, boned and skinned
Two 10¾-ounce cans condensed cream of chicken soup
¼ cup milk
4 slices white bread
Butter

Grease a two-quart casserole or baking dish. Break the salmon into large pieces and arrange on the bottom of the greased casserole. Combine the undiluted cream of chicken soup and ¼ cup of milk; pour over the salmon. Trim crusts off slices of bread, butter the slices and cut them into triangles or circles. Arrange the buttered bread over the top of the casserole mixture. Bake in 400-degree oven for 20 to 30 minutes, or until soup is hot and bread is toasted. Serve hot.

Salmon Crepes Bayou

1 pound salmon flesh, boned, skinned and flaked
1 teaspoon chopped onion
3 tablespoons butter or other fat, melted
¼ cup flour
¼ teaspoon salt
¼ teaspoon white pepper
¼ teaspoon nutmeg
1½ cups milk
2 egg yolks, beaten
2 tablespoons grated Parmesan cheese
2 tablespoons sherry
12 crepes
2 lemon slices, cut into sixths
Parsley

Cook onion in butter until tender. Blend in flour and seasonings. Add milk gradually and cook until thick, stirring constantly. Stir a little of the hot sauce into egg yolk and add to remaining sauce, stirring constantly. Add cheese and sherry and stir until blended. Mix ½ cup of the sauce with the salmon. Blend well. Reserve remaining sauce to serve with crepes.

To make crepes:

¾ cup sifted flour
¼ teaspoon salt
2 eggs, beaten
1 cup milk

Sift together ingredients. Combine egg and milk. Add gradually to flour and salt, and stir only until batter is smooth. Drop 2 tablespoons of batter onto a hot greased griddle or frying pan. Fry about 2 minutes or until crepe is browned on underside, turn, and fry until the bottom is browned.

Spread about 2 tablespoons of the salmon mixture on each crepe. Roll like a jelly roll. Place crepes on a cookie sheet, 15 X 12 inches. Heat in a 350-degree oven for 10 to 15 minutes. Heat the sauce.

Arrange crepes in a circle in a chafing dish. Garnish each crepe with lemon and parsley. Place sauce in the center of the crepes. Serves six.

Prince Rupert Salmon Pie

1 pound salmon flesh, boned and skinned
¼ cup butter or margarine
¼ cup flour
½ teaspoon thyme
¼ teaspoon pepper
2 cups milk
1 can (4 oz.) of chopped mushrooms, drained
1 tablespoon chopped parsley
1½ cups cooked, drained, chopped broccoli
1 cup pastry mix

Break salmon into large pieces. Melt butter and blend in flour and seasonings. Add salmon liquid gradually and cook until thick and smooth, stirring constantly. Add mushrooms, parsley and salmon. Spread broccoli in a 9-inch pie pan. Pour salmon mixture over broccoli. Prepare pastry mix as directed. Roll dough to form a 10-inch circle. Place dough over salmon mixture. Double edge of pastry over and pinch with fingers to make an upright rim. Cut top to allow steam to escape. Bake in 425-degree oven for 20 to 25 minutes or until brown. Serves six.

Vancouver Salmon Puffs

1½ cups salmon flesh, boned, skinned and flaked
½ teaspoon salt

2 egg yolks
2 stiffly beaten egg whites
1½ cups mashed potatoes
1 tablespoon minced onion
⅛ teaspoon pepper

Combine 2 egg yolks with salmon, potatoes and onions. Add salt
and pepper and fold in stiffly beaten egg whites. Pour mixture into
greased custard cups and bake in 350-degree oven for 30 minutes.
Serves four.

Northumberland Cassoulet

1 pound salmon flesh, boned, skinned and flaked
1 cup uncooked elbow macaroni
1 tablespoon chopped green pepper
1 small clove garlic, finely chopped
1/3 cup butter or other fat, melted
1/3 cup flour
2 teaspoons powdered mustard
¼ teaspoon pepper
2 cups milk
1 cup grated cheese
1 cup cooked lima beans

Cook macaroni as directed on the package. Drain. Cook green
pepper and garlic in butter until tender. Blend in flour and seasonings. Add milk gradually and cook until thick, stirring constantly.
Add cheese and continue cooking until cheese melts, stirring constantly. Arrange half of the macaroni, lima beans, salmon and
sauce in layers in a well-greased, 2-quart casserole. Repeat layers,
and bake in 350-degree oven for 25 to 30 minutes. Serves six.

Prince Edward Island Casserole

1/3 cups chopped onion
¼ cup chopped green pepper
¼ cup diced celery
½ cup sliced mushrooms
¼ cup butter or margarine
3 tablespoons flour
1½ teaspoons salt
¼ teaspoon pepper
1 tall can (1⅔ cups) evaporated milk
1 cup water

1 pound salmon flesh, boned, skinned and flaked
2 cups fresh, frozen or canned peas
2 cups crushed potato chips

Sauté onion, green pepper, celery, and mushrooms in melted butter until lightly browned. Add flour, salt and pepper, and mix well. Gradually stir in evaporated milk, then water and cook until smooth and thickened, stirring constantly.

Arrange layers of salmon, peas, the sauce, and potato chips, in that order, in your buttered 2-quart casserole. Dot with butter. Cover and bake in 375-degree oven for 25 minutes. Uncover and bake 10 minutes longer or until top is brown.

When using individual casseroles, cut cooking time in half. Serves six.

Quick Salmon Casserole

1 pound salmon flesh, boned, skinned and flaked
2 cups riced cooked potatoes
1 teaspoon salt
1/8 teaspoon cayenne
1/4 teaspoon white pepper
2 egg whites
1/2 cup heavy cream

Mix salmon lightly with riced potatoes. Add salt, cayenne and white pepper. Beat egg whites until stiff. Beat cream until stiff fold into beaten egg whites. Turn salmon mixture into greased 2-quart baking dish, and pile egg white-cream mixture around edge of the baking dish. Bake in 400-degree oven for 20 to 25 minutes. If desired, just before serving, fill center with hot cooked vegetables of your choice. Serves four.

Salmon Tetrazzini

4 ounces uncooked spaghetti
2 cups salmon flesh, boned and skinned
2 cups milk
2 tablespoons butter or margarine
2 tablespoons all-purpose flour
1/4 teaspoon salt
1/8 teaspoon pepper
1/8 teaspoon nutmeg
2 tablespoons dry sherry

1 3-oz. can (½ cup) broiled sliced mushrooms, drained
2 tablespoons dry bread crumbs
2 tablespoons grated Parmesan cheese

Cook spaghetti according to package directions and drain. Melt butter or margarine and blend in flour, salt, pepper, and nutmeg. Add milk all at once. Cook over medium heat, stirring constantly, till thick and smooth. Add sherry. Break salmon into large pieces. Stir spaghetti, mushrooms and salmon into milk mixture. Turn into 1-quart casserole. Mix together crumbs and cheese, and sprinkle over top. Bake in 350-degree oven for 35 to 40 minutes. Serves six.

Kinnebago Scalloped Salmon

1 pound salmon flesh, boned, skinned and flaked
2 tablespoons lemon juice
2 tablespoons chopped onion
1½ cups coarse cracker crumbs
½ cup melted butter
½ teaspoon salt
½ teaspoon pepper
1 cup milk or fish broth

Combine salmon, lemon juice and onion. Blend the crumbs, butter and seasonings. Pile in alternate layers in a buttered baking dish and add just enough milk (or fish broth) to moisten the crumbs. Dot with butter and bake in 350-degree oven for about 30 minutes or until nicely browned.

Salmon River Escallop

1 pound salmon flesh, boned, skinned and flaked
½ cup finely diced celery
½ cup finely diced onion
½ cup finely chopped parsley
½ teaspoon freshly ground black pepper
1½ cups coarse cracker crumbs
12 to 14 mushroom caps
3 chopped hard-boiled eggs
3 tablespoons sherry
Salt
1 cup milk
Butter crumbs
Grated Parmesan cheese

Combine the salmon with the crumbs, celery, onion, parsley and pepper. Add the mushroom caps, chopped eggs, sherry and salt to taste. Pile in a buttered baking dish, and add just enough milk to moisten crumbs. Top with buttered crumbs and sprinkle with grated Parmesan cheese. Bake in a 350-degree oven for about 30 minutes, or until nicely browned.

Scalloped Salmon Lisbon

1 pound salmon flesh, boned, skinned and flaked
2 tablespoons lemon juice
2 tablespoons chopped onion
1½ cups coarse cracker crumbs
½ cup melted butter
½ teaspoon salt
½ teaspoon pepper
2 tomatoes, peeled and sliced
Grated garlic
Finely chopped parsley
1 cup tomato juice
Dash of cayenne
Anchovies
Large ripe olives.

Mix together salmon, lemon juice, onion, cracker crumbs, butter, salt and pepper. Alternate layers, in a buttered baking dish, of the salmon mixture and slices of tomato which have been sprinkled with garlic and parsley. Add the dash of cayenne to the tomato juice, and pour just enough juice in to moisten crumbs. Top the dish with anchovies and dot with butter. Bake in a 350-degree oven for about 30 minutes, or until nicely browned. After about 25 minutes of baking, just a few minutes before the dish is done, poke large ripe olives into the crumbs.

Scalloped Salmon Venezia

1 pound salmon flesh, boned, skinned and flaked
½ cup finely diced onion
1 clove garlic, grated
¼ cup finely diced green pepper
1 tablespoon chili powder
Small eggplant
Butter
½ cup chili sauce
2 tablespoons Worcestershire sauce

Dash of Tabasco sauce
2 tablespoons sherry or red wine
1½ cups coarse cracker crumbs
½ cup melted butter
½ teaspoon salt

Mix together salmon, diced onion, grated garlic, diced green pepper, chili powder, butter and salt. Brown eggplant slices in butter. Butter a baking dish. Alternate layers of eggplant, salmon mixture and crumbs in the dish. Dilute chili sauce with Worcestershire sauce, Tabasco and sherry (or red wine), and add just enough to moisten the crumbs. Dot with butter and bake in a 350-degree oven for about 30 minutes, or until nicely browned.

Scalloped Salmon and Lima Beans

½ pound salmon flesh, boned, skinned and flaked
12 ounces canned or frozen lima beans
Milk
4 tablespoons butter or margarine
¼ cup flour
1 teaspoon salt
⅛ teaspoon pepper
½ teaspoon Ac'cent
1 cup milk
1 cup buttered soft bread crumbs

Cook lima beans according to directions on package and drain. Pour cooking water into cup and fill cup with milk. Melt butter or margarine in pan and blend in flour, salt, pepper and Ac'cent. Add contents of cup to pan and stir over low heat until smooth and thickened.

Combine salmon with lima beans in 1-quart casserole. Pour sauce over all, and top with buttered crumbs. Bake in 375-degree oven until crumbs are brown, 15 to 20 minutes. Serves four.

Swedish Salmon Pie

2 pounds salmon flesh, skinned and boned
Salt and pepper
Paprika
½ pound shrimp
2 tablespoons finely chopped onion
3 tablespoons chopped parsley
¼ cup sherry or Madeira

2 cups Sauce Veloute
Rich pie crust
1 beaten egg yolk

Cut salmon into cubes and dust with salt, pepper and paprika. Place the salmon, shrimp, onion and parsley in a casserole. Combine the sherry or Madeira with the sauce and pour over the fish mixture. Put a support in the center to hold up the crust, or else build the fish up in the center and pour the sauce around it. Cover with a rich pastry (it is wise to roll it out about an hour ahead and chill it in the refrigerator). Cut little leaves and decorations from the leftover pastry and decorate the crust. Brush well with beaten egg yolk and bake in a 450-degree oven for 15 minutes. Reduce the heat to 375 degrees and cook for another 10 to 15 minutes, or until the top is nicely browned.

Humboldt Pie

2 pounds salmon flesh, boned and skinned
2 tablespoons bottled sweet relish
1 teaspoon salt
¼ teaspoon pepper
2 teaspoons minced onion
¼ cup chopped green pepper
1 teaspoon lemon juice
3 cups packaged crisp rice cereal
1¼ cups milk
2 eggs
2 packages refrigerated crescent dinner rolls
6 green pepper strips
1 egg yolk, slightly beaten
1 cup commercial sour cream

Break salmon into small pieces. In large bowl, combine salmon, sweet relish, salt, pepper, minced onion, green pepper, lemon juice, rice cereal, and milk, and mix well.

In a small bowl with electric mixer, beat eggs until foamy, and fold into salmon mixture. Pour into a well-greased 7-cup shallow baking dish. Bake 35 minutes.

About 5 minutes before salmon is done, remove dough from 1 package crescent rolls. Reroll dough into 2 rectangular pieces. Lay them, side by side, on lightly floured surface, with long sides overlapping ⅛ inch. With fingers, press lightly along overlapping seam to seal sides, forming a large rectangle about 13 x 7 inches.

Do the same with the second package of crescent rolls. Gently lift and place this second large rectangle on top of the first one. Then, with a small spatula, press top of dough gently to remove any visible perforations it may have.

Trim this prepared rectangle into an oval, about one inch smaller than top of baking dish, leaving trimmings in place. Remove baking dish from oven. Gently lift oval-shaped dough onto top of salmon. Cut little leaves and decorations from the left-over pastry and decorate the crust. Garnish exposed salmon mixture with pepper strips.

Brush dough, on top of pie, with beaten egg yolk. Return to 375-degree oven and bake for 10 to 13 minutes or until top is golden. Then top with an oval sheet of foil, one inch larger all around than top of baking dish. Bake 15 minutes longer or until dough tests done with a cake tester.

Serve the salmon pie piping hot, and pass sour cream to top it with. Serves 7 or 8.

Prince of Wales Salmon Pie

First, prepare pie crust:

2 cups enriched flour
3 teaspoons baking powder
½ teaspoon salt
¼ cup margarine or butter
⅔ cup milk

Sift and measure flour. Resift with baking powder and salt. Cut in margarine or butter. Add milk and toss lightly with fork. Knead lightly on floured pastry cloth until smooth on one side. Roll out ¼ inch thick. Fit into baking dish.

To prepare the filling:

3 tablespoons chopped onion
¼ cup chopped green pepper
¼ cup margarine or butter
3 tablespoons enriched flour
2½ cups canned tomatoes
¼ teaspoon salt
⅛ teaspoon pepper
2 teaspoons sugar
1 pound salmon flesh, boned, skinned and flaked
Grated cheese

Sauté onion and green pepper in margarine or butter. Blend in flour. Add tomatoes, seasonings, and sugar, and cook for 15 minutes. Spread salmon on top of biscuit dough. Cover with tomato sauce. Bake in 400-degree oven for 20 to 25 minutes. Sprinkle with cheese. Serves six.

Montreal Salmon Mousse

1 pound salmon flesh, boned and skinned
3 egg whites
1 cup heavy cream
Salt and pepper
Nutmeg
Cayenne
Finely chopped fresh dill

Chop salmon or put it through a fine grinder. The preferred method is to grind it and then pound it in a or work it with a heavy wooden spoon. Place the bowl with the fish over cracked ice and gradually beat in the egg whites, using a whisk or wooden spoon to smooth the fish and make it absorb all the liquid. Then gradually stir in the cream, making sure every bit of it is absorbed as you work it in. Add salt, pepper, and a little nutmeg —you may add cayenne and/or finely chopped fresh dill if you wish. Let it stand over the ice for an hour.

Butter a fish mold and stir the mixture thoroughly before pouring it into the mold. Cover it with waxed paper or buttered brown paper and place it in a pan with about 1 inch of hot water. Bake in 350-degree oven for 25 minutes or until the mousse is firm.

Serve with Sauce Mousseline, Sauce Bechamel, with shrimp or lobster added, or Cucumber Sauce. Tiny new potatoes and sliced cucumber salad are excellent accompaniments.

Kenai Salmon Soufflé

4 tablespoons butter
3 tablespoons flour
¾ cup milk
Salt
1 cup salmon flesh, boned, skinned and flaked
Juice of ½ lemon
6 eggs, separated
½ teaspoon tarragon, or a pinch of fresh dill

Make a heavy cream sauce with the butter, flour and milk.

Season to taste. Add the salmon, lemon juice and the dill or tarragon and let it cool for a few minutes. Gradually add 5 of the 6 egg yolks, slightly beaten. Beat the egg white until stiff and fold them into the mixture. Pour into a buttered soufflé dish. Bake in 375-degree oven for 35 to 45 minutes or until lightly browned. Serve with Sauce Hollandaise. Use the extra egg yolk in making this sauce.

Quick Salmon Soufflé

1 can condensed mushroom or cream of celery soup
1½ cups salmon flesh, boned, skinned and flaked
5 egg yolks
6 egg whites
Butter

Combine the undiluted soup with the salmon and egg yolks, slightly beaten. Taste for seasoning. (You may use smoked salmon, but if you do, do not use any additional salt without tasting first). Fold in the stiffly beaten egg whites and pour the mixture into a buttered souffle dish. Bake in 375-degree oven for 35 to 45 minutes.

Salmon Pilaf

2 large onions, chopped
4 tablespoons butter
1 cup rice
1½ pounds salmon flesh, boned and skinned
Fish broth or white wine to cover
1 tablespoon curry powder
1½ teaspoon salt

Break salmon into small pieces. Saute the chopped onion in butter. Add the rice and cook 5 minutes or until lightly browned. Place in a casserole or baking dish with salmon. Cover to 1 inch above the mixture with fish broth or white wine that has been brought to a boil with the curry powder. If the liquid is not salted, season to taste.

Bake in 350-degree oven, covered, for about 45 minutes, or until the rice is tender and the liquid completely absorbed. If the liquid is absorbed before the rice is cooked, add more. Serve with chutney, crisp fried onions, and chopped almonds.

Role De Saumon

1½ pounds salmon flesh, boned and skinned
½ cup olive or peanut oil or melted butter
4 tablespoons grated onion
3 tablespoons chopped parsley
Salt and pepper
Biscuit dough
Sauce Hollandaise

Cut salmon into thin strips of 3 inches long. Mix the salmon strips well with the shortening and flavorings. Prepare the biscuit dough and roll out to ¼ inch thickness. Spread it with the seasoned fish, roll and secure the ends. Slash the top diagonally. Bake in 375-degree for 30 to 35 minutes or until the roll is nicely browned and cooked through. Serve with Sauce Hollandaise.

VARIATION: Roll and butter the biscuit dough. Cover with paper-thin slices of smoked salmon and sprinkle with freshly ground pepper and lemon juice. Roll and cut in thin wheels. Bake in 425-degree oven until nicely browned, about 15 minutes. They are delicious with cocktails.

Coulibiac of Salmon

This unusual Russian salmon roll is great for buffet service, for it slices well and is easy to eat with a fork. For the crust, use either a bread recipe or the following brioche recipe:

1 yeast cake or envelope yeast
1 tablespoon sugar
⅔ cup milk
4 or more cups flour
4 eggs
4 ounces butter
⅛ teaspoon salt

Dissolve the yeast and sugar in a little warm milk. Mix this with 2 cups of flour and additional milk to make a sponge. Set in a warm place to rise until double in bulk.

Mix the additional flour, the eggs, melted butter and salt with the sponge. Knead it for about 10 minutes or until it is satiny and smooth. Use the dough hook on an electric mixer if you have one. Set it aside in a warm place to rise again.

Now for the filling:

2 pounds salmon fillets cut into small strips
½ pound cod or sole cut into strips
5 tablespoons butter
Salt and pepper
6 shallots
½ pound mushrooms
4 tablespoons butter
Paprika
Chives
Fennel
1 cup buckwheat groats or rice
1 egg
2 cups rapidly boiling water
3 tablespoons butter
3 hard-boiled eggs
1 egg for brushing dough

Sauté the strips of fish lightly in butter for about 2 minutes. Salt and pepper to taste. Sauté the shallots and mushrooms, and add the herbs and seasonings. Mix the buckwheat with a slightly beaten egg, place in a skillet over medium heat and stir until each kernel is separate. Add the boiling water, cover tightly, and let steam for 20 minutes over very low heat.

Roll out the bread or brioche dough to a 14 by 20 inch oblong about ½ inch thick. Butter the dough and place layers of fish, buckwheat, sliced hard-boiled eggs and seasonings in the center. Then fold it over and tuck in the ends so that the dough seals in the mixture. Brush with beaten egg, sprinkle with crumbs and paprika, and let rise in a warm place for 20 to 30 minutes. Bake in 375-degree oven for 30 to 40 minutes or until nicely browned and cooked through.

Slice at the table, and for a thoroughly decadent czarist touch, top with Imperial Russian Sauce, or, if you prefer, with melted butter and chopped parsley.

NOTE: This may be prepared with boiled rice instead of the buckwheat kasha. Add chopped parsley and butter to the rice before mixing it with the fish.

Stuffed Turbans De Saumon

6 salmon steaks (about 6 oz. each), boned and skinned
3 fillets of sole (about 1½ lbs.)

2 tablespoons vegetable oil
Butter or margarine
⅛ teaspoon salt
⅛ teaspoon pepper
Sauce Bernaise
Parsley

Form each steak into a firm round. Cut fillet of sole into six
1-to-1½-inch strips. Wrap a fillet strip around each of the 6 steaks
and secure with toothpicks in about 3 places. Spread the vegetable oil on the bottom of a 12¾ x 9 x 2-inch baking dish, and
place salmon steaks in the dish. Dot each steak with butter and
sprinkle with salt and pepper. Place in 375-degree oven and bake
25 minutes. Baste steaks occasionally with some of the juices in
the dish. Prepare Sauce Bearnaise. Remove steaks from oven.
Preheat broiler. Place steaks about 3 inches from heat and broil
until lightly browned, about 10 to 12 minutes. Place steaks on a
large heated platter and remove toothpicks. Top each with some
of the Sauce Bearnaise and garnish with parsley. Serves six.

Salmon Turbans Hollandaise

1½ pounds salmon flesh, boned, skinned and flaked
3 tablespoons butter or margarine
3 tablespoons flour
1 cup milk
½ teaspoon salt
1 teaspoon lemon juice
1 teaspoon Worcestershire sauce
2 egg yolks, slightly beaten
1½ cups soft bread crumbs
1½ pounds sole fillets
Flour
2 tablespoons vegetable oil
Butter or margarine
Sauce Hollandaise

Melt butter in saucepan over moderate low heat, and blend
in the 3 tablespoons flour. Gradually add milk and cook, stirring
constantly, until it is thickened. Stir in salt, lemon juice and Worcestershire sauce. Remove from heat. Blend a small portion of
sauce into the 2 slightly beaten egg yolks and return to sauce in
saucepan. Add salmon and soft bread crumbs. Spread mixture on
a flat tray, cover, and chill for about an hour.
Divide chilled mixture into 6 portions. Shape each with hands

into a patty about 1 to 1½ inches thick. Cut sole fillets into six 1-to-1½-inch strips. Wrap a strip around each of the patties and secure with toothpicks in about 3 places. Roll lightly in flour. Shake off excess. Spread oil on the bottom of a 12¾ x 9 x 2-inch baking dish, and place salmon patties in the dish. Dot each with butter. Bake in 350-degree oven for 25 minutes. If patties seem dry, brush with more butter during baking. When patties have completed baking, set oven to broil. Broil patties 4 to 5 inches from heat until lightly browned, 10 minutes. Remove toothpicks. Serve immediately with Sauce Hollandaise. Serves six.

Cream and Vermouth Salmon

1 cup dry vermouth
½ cup chopped onions
1 tablespon chopped fresh dill
1 tablespoon prepared horseradish, or ¼ teaspoon dried horse-
    radish
1 tablespoon lemon juice
1 cup heavy cream
Salt and pepper
4 salmon steaks

Simmer vermouth, onion, dill, horseradish and lemon juice in a covered pot for 1 hour. Remove from heat and stir in heavy cream. Season with salt and pepper. Arrange salmon slices in a shallow baking dish and cover with sauce. Bake in 400-degree oven until flesh is cooked through but juicy.

Salmon Miramichi

1 salmon, 10 to 12 pounds
1 pound shrimp
½ cup wild rice
1 tablespoon chopped green pepper
1 small mild onion, chopped
4 tablespoons butter or margarine
Salt and pepper
2 cups cashew nuts
½ cup soft butter or margarine
1 cup fine bread crumbs
1 cup freshly grated processed Swiss cheese
Juice of 1½ lemons
¼ cup dry white wine
½ pint (1 cup) sour cream

Place cleaned whole salmon in a broiling pan on a large piece of cheesecloth. Add 2 cups water to pan and boil over two burners until underside skin may be easily peeled off. Peel, and turn salmon by rolling it over in cheesecloth and repeat for other side. Pull out fin bones and eyes. Hold four ends of cheesecloth and lift salmon from pan to drainboard.

Wash, dry and grease pan liberally with butter. Return fish to greased broiling pan (without rack) by rolling it carefully from cheesecloth. Boil shrimp for 15 minutes.

Boil wild rice according to directions on package, until it is tender. Sauté green pepper and onion in butter. Peel and clean shrimp and cut into pieces if large. Mix shrimp, wild rice, onion, green pepper and butter together, testing for salt, and season with salt and pepper. Stuff mixture into salmon and truss on its side with skewers. Lay salmon on its side. Grind cashew nuts in a food grinder, mix with soft butter, fine bread crumbs and grated cheese. Mix to a smooth paste and spread over the salmon. This mixture should become crusty during baking. Bake in 300-degree oven until fish becomes cooked through but remains juicy. The baking time depends on the size of the salmon, but at least 30 minutes should be allowed. Mix wine, sour cream, and cayenne, and 20 minutes before salmon is done, pour this into pan, stirring it into drippings from salmon (do not baste). Serve from broiling pan, but cover it with aluminum foil and decorate with a garnish. Serves 8.

Broiled whole potatoes, whole parsley and lemon slices can be used for garnish, arranging them in a decorative pattern around covered pan. Put a sliced stuffed olive in the eye socket for effect. This recipe is one of the finest for this great gamefish, so prepare it carefully.

Sour Dill Salmon

Dill and sour cream were made for each other and for salmon, as one taste of this dish will tell you.

1 salmon fillet (about 4 pounds)
Salt and pepper
½ pint commercial sour cream
1 egg yolk
1½ teaspoons minced fresh dill, dill weed, or dill seed

Place salmon, skin side down, on a greased shallow baking pan. Sprinkle lightly with salt and pepper. Bake uncovered in a

400-degree oven for about 15 minutes, or until it will flake. It should not be cooked a minute longer than necessary. Mix sour cream with egg yolk and dill. Remove salmon from oven, spread with sour cream mixture, and put back in the oven for about 5 minutes. Serves 8 to 12.

Moosehead Lake Salmon Steaks

4 salmon steaks
2 tablespoons lemon juice
2 teaspoons instant minced onion
½ teaspoon salt
⅛ teaspoon pepper
¼ cup dairy sour cream
1 teaspoon grated lemon peel
½ teaspoon dried dillweed

Place steaks in a lightly greased baking dish. Combine lemon juice and onion, and sprinkle over salmon. Season with salt and pepper. Bake, uncovered, in 400-degree oven for 15 to 20 minutes or until fish flakes easily. Remove from oven, and spread sour cream over salmon. Sprinkle with lemon peel and dill. Return to oven and bake 3 minutes longer. Serve with lemon wedges. Makes 4 servings.

Salmon Pasta

½ pound salmon flesh, boned, skinned and flaked
1 pound ricotta cheese
12 large pasta shells
3 quarts boiling water
1 tablespoon salt
3 tablespoons butter or margarine
3 tablespoons flour
½ teaspoon salt
¼ teaspoon pepper
¼ teaspoon nutmeg
1 cup milk
1 cup cooked, drained spinach
½ cup grated Parmesan cheese
Parsley

Add salmon and cheese together and mix well. Cook pasta shells in boiling salted water for 45 minutes or until tender. Drain. Rinse with water to remove excess starch. Melt butter, and blend in flour and seasonings. Add milk gradually and cook until thick and smooth, stirring constantly. Chop spinach. Add spinach and blend thoroughly. An electric mixer or blender may be used. Pour sauce into a well-greased baking dish, 8 x 8 x 2 inches. Fill pasta shells with salmon mixture and arrange over spinach. Sprinkle with cheese. Bake in 350-degree oven for 30 minutes. Garnish with parsley. Serves six.

Killarney Salmon Tart

1 pound salmon flesh, boned, skinned, and flaked
1 cup pastry mix
½ cup chopped onion
2 tablespoons butter or margarine, melted
2 tablespoons chopped parsley
4 eggs, beaten
1½ cups coffee cream
½ teaspoon salt

Prepare pastry mix as directed on package. Roll and line a 9-inch pie pan. Spread salmon in pie shell. Cook onion in butter until tender. Sprinkle parsley and onion over salmon. Combine eggs, cream and salt. Pour over salmon. Bake in 350-degree oven for 35 to 45 minutes or until pie is firm in center. Serves six.

Willow Creek Salmon Box

3 cups steamed rice
3 cups cold boiled salmon flesh, boned, skinned and flaked
1 tablespoon salt
¼ teaspoon pepper
⅛ teaspoon nutmeg

Butter a bread pan well and line it with half of the steamed rice. Season the salmon flesh. Pour it over the rice, sprinkle with combined salt, pepper and nutmeg and cover with remaining rice. Cover and bake in a 350-degree oven for 30 minutes.

Meanwhile, prepare this cup of egg sauce:

2 hard-boiled eggs, chopped or diced
1 cup Thick White Sauce

Prepare the Thick White Sauce with 3 tablespoons of flour rather than 4, and add the hard-boiled eggs. If you like, you may add 2 tablespoons of chopped capers, too.

When the salmon is done, turn it out onto a hot platter, pour the egg sauce over it, and serve.

Pennsylvania Dutch Salmon

In olden times, salmon was a mainstay during the cold winter months, and Pennsylvania Dutch homemakers kept a plentiful supply of it on hand in dried, smoked and salted forms. Since the 17th Century, when William Penn wooed settlers from their Palatinate and Upper Rhine homelands in Germany, the following has been one of their favorite ways of preparing fresh salmon.

2⅓ cups cooked rice
2 tablespoons melted butter
1 pound salmon flesh, boned, skinned and flaked
1 cup grated Swiss cheese
3 eggs
1 cup milk
¼ teaspoon salt
¼ teaspoon freshly ground pepper
Cherry tomatoes

Combine rice and butter. Line a 1-quart baking dish with rice, pressing it evenly over bottom and sides of the dish. Sprinkle half the cheese over the rice, top with salmon, then remaining cheese.

Beat the eggs lightly and stir in the milk and seasonings. Pour over the salmon cheese mixture. Bake in 400-degree oven for 20 to 30 minutes, or until a knife inserted in the center comes out clean.

Garnish with cherry tomatoes. Serves eight.

11
Broiled Salmon

Quick Broiled Salmon

The procedure is the same whether this is done over charcoal or under gas or electric flame. The fish should be about 2 inches from the heat source.

If you relish an herb flavor, you will find that rosemary, dill or tarragon are all delicious when cooked with salmon. Rub in a little of the herbs before you oil the fish. Brush the steaks or fillets well with oil and squirt with a little lemon juice. Place the fish in an oiled, preheated broiling pan, and broil for about 5 minutes. Baste the fish with the oil in the pan, turn, and broil for about 5 minutes more, or until the fish flakes easily when tested with a fork. Salt and pepper and remove to a hot platter, serving with plenty of lemon. Plain boiled potatoes and cucumber salad are flattering accompaniments.

If you prefer a rich sauce with the already rich salmon, you can serve a Sauce Hollandaise or Sauce Béarnaise.

Salmon En Brochette

2 pounds salmon flesh, boned and skinned
4 tablespoons lemon juice
Fresh dill or dill pickles
1 teaspoon salt
½ teaspoon pepper
1 pound mushrooms
½ cup olive or peanut oil

Cut salmon into 1½-inch cubes, mix well with seasonings and let stand for 3 to 6 hours. When ready to broil it, place a mushroom cap on the end of each skewer, then 2 salmon cubes, another mushroom, more salmon, and end with a mushroom cap. Brush well with oil and broil, turning several times during the process, or bake in 375-degree oven, basting with the marinade. Serve with plain boiled potatoes and fresh dill or dill potatoes.

Charcoaled Salmon Steaks

6 salmon steaks
1½ teaspoons salt
1½ teaspoons black pepper
1 teaspoon paprika
6 tablespoons soft butter

Get the charcoal fire going well, but wait until it subsides to glowing embers before you begin cooking, unless you want to scorch the fish and taste nothing but charcoal.

Season both sides of salmon steaks generously with salt, pepper and paprika. Use half the butter to cover one side of the steaks well. Broil them 3 inches from the coals, buttered side up, for 4 minutes. Turn the steaks, spread the other side with butter and broil another 4 minutes. Serve immediately on hot plates.

If you would like to add more flavor and interest to the dish, melt another 3 tablespoons of butter, blend in 6 chopped green olives, 6 chopped black olives and ¼ bud finely minced garlic, and pour it over the charcoaled steaks.

12
Boiled Salmon

Ketchikan Salmon Rolls

1 cup stale bread crumbs
½ teaspoon salt
Few grains pepper
1 cup milk
2 cups salmon flesh, boned, skinned and flaked
Few grains nutmeg
1 teaspoon chopped parsley
3 eggs
Grate rind of 1 lemon
1 teaspoon lemon juice

Mix bread crumbs, salt, pepper and milk, stirring mixture until it becomes a paste. Add fish, nutmeg, chopped parsley and eggs, and mash until smooth. Add lemon rind and juice, and mix well. Roll mixture into little sausage shapes. Drop them into a pot of boiling water, cover, and simmer for 30 minutes. Serve hot or cold, with Sauce Mayonnaise.

Chef-Style Salmon Italienne

2 pounds salmon flesh, boned and skinned
3 quarts water
½ teaspoon salt
8 peppercorns
½ cup vinegar
1 medium onion, sliced
2 tablespoons wine vinegar
4 tablespoons olive oil
1 teaspoon chopped parsley

1 tablespoon capers
3 tiny sour pickles, sliced

Cut salmon into cubes, and boil them in water with salt, pepper-corns, vinegar and onion, for 20 minutes, or until tender. Remove from fire and drain.

Mix vinegar, oil, parsley, capers and pickles together and pour over boiled fish. Serves four.

Scottish Salmon Kedgeree

1 pound salmon flesh, boned, skinned and flaked
4 hard-boiled eggs
2 cups cooked rice
¼ cup chopped parsley
1½ cups Sauce Béchamel
1½ tablespoons curry powder

Mix curry powder with Sauce Bechamel. Place alternate layers of rice, fish, eggs, parsley and Bechamel in the top of a double boiler or in a mold. Place over hot water and heat thoroughly. You may wish to serve additional Béchamel with curry as an accompanying sauce.

VARIATION: You may omit the curry and use tomato sauce spiced with chili powder instead. Or, rather than the Béchamel, you can use heavy cream—just enough to moisten the mixture.

Ouananiche Shortcake

3 cups Medium White Sauce
1 cup freshly grated cheese
½ cups salmon flesh, boned, skinned and flaked
1 cup cooked peas
1 tablespoon lemon juice
Baking powder biscuit dough

Make the White Sauce, add cheese, salmon, peas and lemon juice, and heat thoroughly.

Make baking powder biscuit dough and bake in a round cake pan. Split and serve hot salmon mixture as a filling and topping for biscuit shortcake. Or serve on split hot biscuits, or on toasted bread. Serves six.

Tanana Salmon Dish

2 cups cooked or canned tomatoes and juice
¼ cup diced onion

¼ cup diced green pepper, or celery
2 tablespoons bacon fat, or meat drippings
1½ cups boiling water
Salt and pepper
1/3 cup uncooked rice
¼ cup chopped olives, if desired
2 cups salmon flesh, boned, skinned and flaked

Combine tomatoes, onion, green pepper, fat, water, salt and pepper in a large saucepan. Bring to a boil. (2½ cups of raw tomatoes, cut into pieces, may be used instead of 2 cups cooked). Add rice and simmer until rice is tender, about 20 to 25 minutes, adding more water if needed. Add olives and salmon and cook 2 or 3 minutes longer to blend flavors. Serves six.

Norwegian Creamed Salmon

6 tablespoons butter or margarine
6 tablespoons minced onion
7 tablespoons flour
2 cups milk
Salt and pepper
¾ cup heavy cream
½ cup sherry
¼ cup brandy
1½ pounds fresh salmon, poached and flaked
2 tablespoons minced parsley

Melt the butter in a saucepan, and saute the minced onion until transparent, but not browned. Stir in the flour, making sure it blends in well. Bring the milk to a boil in another pan. Stirring vigorously all the while, add the hot milk to the butter and onion mixture, stirring until the sauce is smooth and thick. Stir in the salt and pepper. Reduce the heat, and add the cream, sherry and brandy. Do not allow to boil after the cream is in the sauce. Stir in the flaked salmon and minced parsley, and heat over low flame until salmon is hot through. Serve over toast.

Bristol Bay Creamed Salmon

2 tablespoons butter or margarine
4 tablespoons flour
¾ teaspoon salt
⅛ teaspoon pepper
1 teaspoon sugar
2 cups milk

¾ cup salmon flesh, boned, skinned and flaked
1½ cups cooked or canned whole kernel corn
1 tablespoon chopped pimento

Melt butter or margarine, and blend in flour, salt, pepper and sugar. Gradually add milk. Cook over hot water, stirring constantly, until thick. Add salmon, corn, and pimento. Serve over toast. Serves four.

Salmon Baranoff

3 pounds of salmon fillet
3 cups wine
2 cups water
3 medium carrots
2 onions
1 small bay beef
Salt and pepper
3 tablespoons butter
5 cups cooked pureed spinach
3 tablespoons heavy cream
3 egg yolks
1 tablespoon flour

Place salmon in a heavy saucepan with wine, carrots, water, onions, and bay beef. Add a tablespoon of butter, cover the pan, and simmer for 40 minutes, or until salmon flakes easily when tested with a fork. Do not overcook. Drain salmon, reserving the cooking liquid.

Combine the spinach and the cream, and heat. Stir in the egg yolks, and continue to cook over medium heat for 5 minutes, or until spinach is hot. Arrange a layer of spinach on the bottom of a heated serving dish. Arrange the salmon on top in serving portions. Keep warm. Melt the rest of the butter, add the flour, and stir in a cup of the liquid in which the salmon was cooked. Heat until smooth and thick, pour over salmon, and serve immediately.

Rice Salmon Delmonico

1 pound salmon flesh, boned, skinned and flaked
¼ cup of butter or margarine
¼ cup flour
1½ teaspoons salt
⅛ teaspoon white pepper
¼ teaspoon cayenne

2 cups milk
1 egg yolk, slightly beaten
2 tablespoons lemon juice
2 tablespoons sherry
8 ounces sliced mushrooms, drained
3 cups hot cooked rice
1 hard-boiled egg, sliced

Melt butter in saucepan, and stir in flour, salt, pepper and cayenne. Add milk all at once, stirring constantly until smooth. Cook until thickened, stirring occasionally. Add some of the hot sauce to egg yolk and mix thoroughly. Return to saucepan and add lemon juice and sherry. Cook until thickened. Fold in salmon and mushrooms. Heat thoroughly. Serve over the rice, garnished with the hard-boiled egg slices. Serves six.

Quick Salmon Curry

1 medium onion, finely chopped
3 tablespoons butter
1 cup salmon flesh, boned, skinned and flaked
1 can green pea or cream of celery soup
1½ tablespoons curry powder
Heavy cream, vermouth or white wine

Saute the onion in butter until lightly browned. Add salmon, soup and curry powder, and blend well. Heat to the boiling point. If the mixture is too thick, add several tablespoons of cream or vermouth or white wine. Serve with rice and chutney.

Chinese Salmon And Onions

½ pound cooked salmon, boned and skinned
1 large onion
2 eggs
1 tablespoon parsley, chopped
Salt and pepper

Cut the onion up into small pieces and fry in a little fat. Shred the salmon into thin strips and add to the onions, cooking for one minute. Beat the eggs, yolk and white together, and add seasoning. Pour over salmon and onions and keep stirring all the time. Cook for one additional minute. Garnish with chopped parsley.

13
Poached Salmon

New England Boiled Salmon

1 salmon (4 to 6 pounds)
Salt
3 peppercorns
1 bay beef
2 slices lemon

Clean and wash salmon, and wrap it in a piece of cheesecloth, leaving the ends long enough so that you can easily lift it in and out of the pan. Heat 2 to 3 quarts of water mixed with salt and other seasonings. Bring it to the boiling point and let it boil for 15 minutes. Reduce the heat until the water is barely simmering, add salmon and simmer it for 15 to 20 minutes, or until it flakes easily. It usually takes 6 to 8 minutes per pound. Do not over-cook, or it will become mushy.

Serve the salmon with egg sauce:

2 cups Sauce Béchamel
2 hard-boiled eggs, chopped

Mix coarsely chopped hard-boiled eggs with the Sauce Bechamel. If you like, make your Béchamel with some of the fish stock. Garnish the platter with parsley and lemon slices.

Accompany salmon with small new potatoes, cooked in boiling water until just tender, then drenched with butter, salt, pepper, and a good sprinkling of chopped parsley and with cooked, buttered peas.

Salmon Steaks Espagnol

8 salmon steaks
1½ cups milk
1½ cups water
Juice of 1 lemon
Sauce Hollandaise

Place the steaks in a large saucepan, salting lightly. Add the milk, water and lemon juice, and poach gently for 13 minutes. Fish is done when it flakes easily. Serve on hot plates with a tablespoon of hot Sauce Hollandaise over each steak.

Poached Salmon In Aspic

2 cups dry white wine
2 cups water
½ teaspoon oregano
1 small onion
1 bay beef
1 clove
1 carrot, sliced thin
3 sprigs parsley
1 clove garlic, sliced
⅛ teaspoon celery salt
Salt and pepper
4 salmon steaks
1 slightly beaten egg white
1 crushed egg shell
2 envelopes unflavored gelatin
½ cup cold water

Boil the wine, water, spices and vegetables together for 10 minutes. Add the salmon steaks, and cook over low heat until the salmon is done, turning the fish once. The pieces should be ready in about 10 minutes. Don't overcook them. Remove the salmon from the stock and chill. Strain the stock, add the egg white and the egg shell, boil two minutes, then strain through a clean linen napkin. Soften the gelatin in the ½ cup cold water, and add it to the stock. Heat gently until the gelatin has dissolved, then chill until almost set. Spoon some of the thickened gelatin mixture over the bottom of the serving platter, which should be cold. Arrange the salmon on the gelatin, then cover with the remaining aspic. Chill until the aspic is quite firm, about 3 or 4 hours. Garnish with hard-boiled eggs, lettuce and cold cooked vegetables. Serve with Green Mayonnaise Sauce.

14
Braised Salmon

Braised Salmon In Chablis

3 large white onions, thinly sliced
3 large carrots, thinly sliced
2 stalks celery, chopped
1 clove garlic, thinly sliced
2 small bay leaves
3 sprigs parsley
1 sprig tarragon
1 sprig marjoram
3 tablespoons butter or margarine
1 salmon (5 to 7 pounds)
½ teaspoon salt
8 peppercorns
6 strips bacon
1 bottle Chablis

Saute onions, carrots, celery, garlic, bay leaves, parsley, tarragon and majoram in 3 tablespoons of butter for 5 minutes. Arrange in the bottom of a large baking dish and place the salmon on top. Sprinkle with salt and scatter on the peppercorns. Place the strips of bacon across the top of the fish. Pour enough of the white wine to half-cover the fish. Cover the pan and bake in a 350-degree oven for 35 minutes. Serve with another bottle of chilled Chablis, creamed diced potatoes and side dishes of cooked fresh spinach drenched in red-wine vinegar.

Braised Salmon Bourguignon Rouge

2 medium onions, thinly sliced
2 stalks celery, cut into strips
1 carrot, cut into thin strips

3 sprigs parsley
1 leek, cut into strips
5 tablespoons butter or margarine
1 salmon (6 to 8 pounds)
Salt
1 quart (or more) red wine
1 teaspoon thyme
1 bay leaf
18 small white onions
3 tablespoons butter or margarine
1 pound mushrooms

Place onions, celery, carrot, parsley and leek in the bottom of a large fish cooker or braising pan with 5 tablespoons butter and let cook over a medium flame until wilted down. Salt the salmon inside and out and place it on this bed of vegetables. Add red wine to half the height of the fish in the pan and put in the thyme and bay leaf. Let it just come to a boil. Cover the fish with a piece of cooking parchment and place it in the oven for about 40 minutes or until the salmon is cooked through. Meanwhile, brown the small onions in 3 tablespoons of butter and let them cook through in a covered pan. Saute the mushrooms lightly in butter and season to taste.

Baste the fish in the oven from time to time. When it is cooked, arrange it on a hot platter and surround it with the onions and mushrooms. Strain the sauce, and if you wish it thickened add beurre manière (make by kneading 2 tablespoons of butter with 3 tablespoons of flour). Taste for seasoning and serve it separately.

Braised Salmon Bourguignon Blanc

First, place the following vegetables in the bottom of a large fish cooker or braising pan with the butter and cook them over a medium flame until wilted down:

2 medium onions, thinly sliced
2 stalks celery, cut into strips
1 carrot, cut into thin strips
3 sprigs parsley
1 leek, cut into strips
5 tablespoons butter

Next, prepare this bread stuffing:

¾ cup melted butter or margarine
2 tablespoons grated onion
4 cups breadcrumbs or cubes

1 teaspoon salt
¼ teaspoon pepper
2 tablespoons lemon juice
2 tablespoons chopped parsley
2 teaspoons capers

Add onion and crumbs to melted butter. Stir over low heat until crumbs brown slightly. Add and mix remaining ingredients. If desired, ½ teaspoon sage or thyme may be substituted for capers.

Now ready the following:

1 salmon (6 to 8 pounds)
White wine
½ pound mushrooms, sauted in butter
1 pound shrimp
1 cup cream
Beurre manière

Clean and wash the salmon and stuff with bread stuffing, sewing it or securing with skewers and twine. Place the salmon on the bed of vegetables and add white wine to half the salmon's height. Baste the salmon frequently as it is baking, and about 5 minutes before it is done add the shrimp to the pan juices. When the salmon flakes easily, remove it to a hot platter and surround it with the shrimp and the sautéed mushrooms.

Strain the pan juices and reduce to 1 cup. Add the cream and thicken with beurre manière (make by kneading 2 tablespoons butter with 3 tablespoons flour). Serve with salmon.

Braised Salmon À L'Americaine

First you must prepare Shrimp a l'Americaine.

3 pounds shrimp
½ cup olive oil
3 tablespoons butter
1 small onion, finely chopped
6 shallots, finely chopped
1 clove garlic, peeled and chopped
6 ripe tomatoes, peeled, seeded and chopped
3 tablespoons chopped parsley
1 tablespoon chopped fresh tarragon, or 1 teaspoon dried tarragon
1½ teaspoons thyme
½ bay leaf
1½ cups white wine
3 tablespoons tomato puree

Cayenne pepper
Salt
¼ cup cognac

Heat olive oil and add shrimp. Toss the shrimp around in the oil until the meat is seared, then remove it from the oil to a hot platter. Add the butter to the pan with the olive oil and saute the onions and shallots until lightly colored. Add the garlic, the tomatoes, the herbs and white wine and let it simmer for 30 minutes. Add the tomato puree and season to taste. Pour the cognac over the shrimp pieces and ignite. Then put them in the sauce, cover and simmer for about 20 minutes. Remove from the fire and let stand for an hour or so.

Meanwhile, place the following vegetables in the bottom of a large fish cooker or braising pan with the butter and cook them over a medium flame until wilted down:

2 medium onions, thinly sliced
2 stalks celery, cut into strips
1 carrot, cut into thin strips
3 sprigs parsley
1 leek, cut into strips
5 tablespoons butter
Next, prepare the following stuffing:
4 tablespoons butter or margarine
1 tablespoon water
2 teaspoons anchovy paste
2 cups soft bread crumbs
1 cup finely cut cooked shrimp
½ teaspoon grated onion
2 tablespoons lemon juice
4 teaspoons chopped stuffed olives

Heat the butter, water and anchovy paste together until butter is melted. Add to the crumbs and mix in remaining ingredients.

Now ready the following:

1 salmon (6 to 8 pounds)
White wine

Clean and wash the salmon and stuff with your shrimp stuffing, sewing it or securing with skewers and twine. Place the salmon on the bed of vegetables and add white wine to half the salmon's height. Baste the salmon frequently as it is baking. When salmon flakes easily, remove it to a hot platter, surround it with the Shrimp à l'Americaine, and top off with Sauce à l'Americaine. Serve with rice pilaf.

15
Cold Salmon

Steamed Salmon Nova Scotia

1 salmon (about 8 pounds)
12 sprigs fresh dill
1½ cups sour cream
1 cup mayonnaise
Salt and pepper

Put the salmon on a piece of aluminum foil twice as large as the fish. Put half the dill inside the salmon and strew the rest of the dill on top. Bring the foil around the fish so that it's completely enclosed, and transfer to a fish cooker, or to a rack in a large steamer or other pot. Pour an inch of boiling water into the pot—the water must not cover the fish. Put the pot in 325-degree oven, covered, and cook the fish 10 minutes per pound, or until it flakes easily when tested with a fork. Remove from the cooker, and let stand in the foil until cool. Then refrigerate, still in the foil, until entirely cold. It may stand overnight, if necessary or convenient. Just before you wish to serve it, take it out of the foil, trim off the skin, and put the fish on a large platter. Combine the remaining ingredients, and spoon the mixture over the salmon. Garnish with dill sprigs, radish roses, parsley, or other greens, and serve on a bed of crisp dry greens. Serves ten.

Cold Poached Salmon

Cold salmon is the ultimate in summer dining, and a spectacular dish for a buffet supper.

First, prepare this highly spiced court bouillon:

3 quarts water
1 quart white wine

114

1 cup wine vinegar
3 onions
9 cloves
4 carrots, finely cut
2 stalks celery
1 bay leaf
1 teaspoon thyme
4 sprigs parsley
1 tablespoon salt

Stick 3 cloves in each onion. Combine all ingredients and bring to a boil. Simmer for 1 hour before adding salmon.

Clean and wash salmon, and wrap it in cheesecloth so you can lift it from the broiler without breaking it. Allow about 7 minutes per pound of fish when you poach it. When poached through, remove the fish from the bouillon and set the bouillon aside to cool. While the fish is cooling, carefully remove the skin and trim the fish so that it looks inviting. If you are serving a whole fish, you may want to leave on the head and tail, to give it that classical appearance. Arrange your salmon on a large platter and garnish with sliced cucumbers, tiny or sliced tomatoes, parsley, watercress and thin slices of lemon. Serve with one of the following: (3 to 4 parts oil to 1 part vinegar, plus salt and pepper), Sauce Vinaigrette Mayonnaise, Sauce Remoulade, Sauce Tartare, or Sauce Verte.

Salmon steaks may be poached, chilled, and served in the same way. When all of fairly equal size, they make an attractive platter. Of course, they will take much less cooking time than a large piece of fish.

VARIATION: Spiced salmon is another delectable cold dish. After poaching the fish, reduce the court bouillon to half its volume. Flavor to taste with vinegar, herbs and seasonings, pour this over the salmon and let stand for 24 hours. Drain and serve with mayonnaise. The pickle should be highly spiced and quite well laced with vinegar.

Gravad Lax (Swedish Marinated Salmon)

1 salmon (4 to 5 pounds dressed weight), bone removed
⅔ cup salt
½ cup sugar
1 tablespoon coarsely ground black pepper
Bit of saltpeter
Fresh dill

Cut the salmon into two even pieces. Mix the salt, sugar, pepper and saltpeter together and rub the salmon well with this mixture. Line the bottom of a deep pan or casserole with dill branches, place a piece of salmon on them, skin side down. Sprinkle the top with the spices and add more dill sprigs. Place the second piece of salmon on this, skin side up. Put a board and a weight on top and place it in the refrigerator for 24 hours or more.

It is not cooked. The action of the spice and seasonings gives it an unusual texture and a remarkably good flavor. It is excellent sliced thin and served with black bread as a cocktail snack, or a pleasant addition to a luncheon plate of cold meat and salad. It should then be served with a vinaigrette sauce (3 to 4 parts oil to 1 part vinegar, plus salt and pepper).

Pickled Salmon

4 to 5 pounds salmon
2 quarts vinegar
1 ounce peppercorns
1 grated nutmeg
6 blades mace
1 tablespoon salad oil

Wrap the salmon in a fish cloth and simmer in salted water about 45 minutes. Drain, wrap in a dry cloth and set in a cold place until ready to use. For the pickle, use one quart of water in which the salmon was cooked, the vinegar, peppercorns, grated nutmeg, and mace. Boil for a few minutes in a kettle closely covered to prevent evaporation of the flavor. Cool. When quite cold, pour over the salmon, then pour in the oil. Cover closely and place in a dry cool place. This pickle will keep many months.

Saumon Froid Au Chambertin

Whole salmon with head
Red wine court bouillon
3 envelopes gelatin
Salt and pepper

First, prepare the rich red wine court bouillon:

2 pounds fish bones and heads
3 quarts water

1 quart red wine
Bouquet garni (thyme, parsley, leek)
2 stalks celery
1 onion stuck with cloves
3 carrots cut into quarters
1 tablespoon salt

Cook the bones and heads of fish in 2 quarts of water for 30 minutes. Add the remaining water and all the other ingredients and continue cooking for 20 minutes. You may need more bouillon if your salmon is quite large.

Wrap the salmon in cheesecloth or place it on a rack and poach it in bouillon until it flakes easily. This should take about 6 minutes per pound of salmon. Remove salmon carefully to a large board or platter and let it cool. Take off the skin, cutting sharply at the tail and stripping it up to the head.

Reduce the bouillon to about 2 quarts. Clarify it with the white of an egg and shell and strain it through a linen napkin. Dissolve the gelatin in ¾ cup of cold water and prepare an aspic, using 6 cups of the hot bouillon stirred into the gelatin. While the aspic is cooling, prepare the garnishes:

1 cup cooked small peas
1 cup finely cut cooked snap beans
1 cup finely diced cooked carrots
1 cup finely diced cooked potatoes
Mayonnaise
Small tomatoes
Ripe olives
15 hard-boiled eggs
Salt and pepper
Cucumbers, sliced
Lemons, sliced

Mix the cooked vegetables with enough mayonnaise to bind them stiffly. Peel and scoop out the tomatoes and stuff them with the vegetable salad. Brush the tops with a thin layer of the aspic and top each one with a ripe olive. Cut the eggs in half horizontally and remove the yolks. Mash and mix with salt, pepper, chopped ripe olives and mayonnaise. Heap this mixture into the whites, or pipe it through a pastry tube. Glaze the tops with aspic. Brush the salmon with aspic, giving it a thick coating, then let it set thoroughly, and give it another coating. Decorate the salmon with thin cucumber slices, lemon slices, and quarters of ripe olives and hard-boiled egg yolk.

Arrange the platter as elaborately as you like, for this a real show piece. Surround the salmon with the stuffed tomatoes and the stuffed eggs. Serve with either Sauce Mayonnaise, or Sauce Verte.

Salmon Cutlets In Aspic

6 salmon steaks
White wine court bouillon
2 envelopes gelatin
Fresh tarragon leaves
Hard-boiled eggs
Cucumber

First, prepare the rich white wine court bouillon:

1 pound fish bones and heads
1 quart water
1 quart dry white wine
1 teaspoon dried thyme
2 onions stuck with cloves
2 carrots, diced
2 cloves garlic
1 bay leaf
Salt and pepper

Cook fish bones and heads in the water for 30 minutes. Strain through fine cloth. This should give you about a quart of bouillon. Add all the other ingredients, bring to a boil and simmer for 20 minutes, then poach the salmon steaks in it just long enough for them to cook through. Remove them to a dry towel or absorbent paper and take off the skin. Arrange the steaks in a deep platter or in individual serving dishes.

Decorate the steaks with tarragon leaves and hard-boiled eggs, cucumber slices, or any other garnish you prefer. Prepare the aspic by dissolving the gelatin in ½ cup of cold water and combining it with 4 cups of hot clarified bouillon. Allow it to cool. When it is partly congealed, brush the decorated salmon slices with this mixture and place them in the refrigerator to chill. When the glaze is firm, pour enough of the rest of the gelatin mixture over the slices to cover them. Chill until ready to serve. Serve with Sauce Mayonnaise.

Newfoundland Salmon Loaf

4 salmon steaks
White wine court bouillon (2 cups clarified)

1 egg white and shell
1 envelope gelatin
1 cucumber, seeded and cubed
1 medium onion, thinly sliced
12 stuffed olives
3 hard-boiled eggs
2 pimentos cut in strips
Greens

Prepare a rich white wine court bouillon as in the recipe for
SALMON CUTLETS IN ASPIC, and poach the steaks in it
just long enough to cook them through. Then remove the skin,
cool them, and cut them into small cubes. Reduce the bouillon
to 2 cups, clarify it with the egg white and shell, and strain it
through a napkin. Dissolve the gelatin in ¼ cup of cold water
or broth and combine it with the hot bouillon. Let it cool until
it starts to set.

Pour a thin layer of the gelatin mixture into a bread pan or
small mold and put it in the refrigerator to solidify. Arrange
sliced olives, halved hard-boiled eggs and rings of onion on the
bottom of the mold. Toss the salmon cubes with the cubed cucumber, the pimento and more onion rings and arrange this mixture
in the mold. Cover with the remaining gelatin and chill in the
refrigerator. Unmold on a bed of greens and serve with either
Sauce Mayonnaise or Sauce Verte.

Salmon Steaks Parisienne

4 salmon steaks
White wine court bouillon (3½ cups clarified)
1 egg white and shell
2 envelopes gelatin
Asparagus tips
Hard-boiled eggs

Prepare a rich white wine court bouillon as in the recipe for
SALMON CUTLETS IN ASPIC (Chapter 15), and poach
the steaks in it just long enough for them to cook through. Remove to cool. Cook the bouillon down to about 4 cups. Clarify
it with the egg white and shell and strain through a linen napkin.
Dissolve the gelatin in ½ cup of cold water or bouillon and add
the rest of the broth. Let it cool until almost set.

Remove the skin from the salmon steaks. When the jelly is
almost set, combine 1 cup of it with 1½ cups of Sauce Verte.

Give the salmon steaks a liberal coating of this mixture. Spread the jellied bouillon in the bottom of a rather deep platter, arrange the salmon on top of this and decorate with asparagus tips and hard-boiled eggs. Serve with additional Sauce Verte.

Salmon Luncheon Loaf

1 piece salmon, 3 to 4 pounds
3 eggs
1 teaspoon chopped parsley
2 tablespoons flour
Few grains mace
Few grains nutmeg
1 cup milk
1 tablespoon lemon juice
Salt and pepper

Boil fish for 15 minutes. Skin, and then pick flesh from bones. Mash flesh to a paste. Add eggs, parsley, flour, mace and nutmeg. Stir in milk, add lemon juice, season with salt and pepper, and mix thoroughly. Grease a loaf pan, pack in mixture, cover with aluminum foil, and tie down cover. Steam for 1 hour. Chill, and serve with the following sauce:

½ cup mayonnaise
1 small jar whole red caviar
1 tablespoon tiny capers
1 teaspoon grated onion

Mix, and spread over fish loaf. Serves 6 to 8.

Salmon Labrador

1 piece of salmon, 5 pounds
Salt and pepper
1 can crab meat
½ cup mayonnaise
2 tablespoons wine vinegar
1 teaspoon Worcestershire sauce
6 stuffed green olives
1 teaspoon grated lemon rind
Cucumber slices
Parsley

Salt fish and wrap it in cheesecloth. Steam it covered for 30 to 45 minutes. Remove fish to a platter, unwrap, and peel off skin.

Slide cheesecloth from under fish. Chill. Mix crab, mayonnaise, vinegar, Worcestershire sauce, olives and lemon rind. Stuff into chilled fish. Garnish with sliced cucumbers and sprigs of parsley. Serves 6 to 8.

Glacier Bay Chilled Salmon

1 piece salmon, 4 pounds
4 tablespoons Escoffier Sauce Diable
½ teaspoon dry mustard
1 teaspoon chopped chives or minced onion
1 teaspoon lemon juice
1 cup mayonnaise
Salt
Watercress

Tie a piece of salmon in cheesecloth and steam in salted water for 1 hour. Cool and chill, Mix Escoffier Sauce Diable, mustard, chives, lemon juice, and mayonnaise. Taste for salt. Place salmon on cold platter and cover evenly with sauce. Arrange watercress around rim of platter. Serves 6 to 8.

Salmon Mousse With Sour Cream Sauce

3 cups salmon flesh, boned, skinned and flaked
½ tablespoon salt
1½ tablespoons sugar
2 teaspoons flour
1 teaspoon dry mustard
Dash of tabasco sauce
2 egg yolks
2 tablespoons butter
¾ cup milk
¼ cup white vinegar
1 envelope unflavored gelatin
¼ cup water

Mix the salt, sugar, flour, mustard, Tabasco, egg yolks, butter, milk and vinegar in the top of a double boiler. Cook over boiling water, stirring constantly, until mixture thickens. Soften the gelatin in the quarter cup of water, and add it to the hot mixture, stirring until gelatin is all dissolved. Turn off the heat, and gently fold the salmon into the pan, stirring only until well blended. Cool, then pour the mousse into a six-cup mold (preferably one shaped like a fish, of course), and chill until set, about 3 hours.

Meanwhile, make the Sour Cream Sauce:

1 cup sour cream
1 tablespoon white vinegar
2 tablespoons lemon juice
1 teaspoon sugar
Dash of tabasco sauce
1 slice onion
1 cucumber

Combine the sour cream, vinegar, lemon juice, sugar and tabasco. Mince the onion, or chop it very fine, and add it to the sour cream. Peel the cucumber, seed it (you can use a melon ball cutter to scoop out the seeds), and cut the remaining shell into small bits. Fold these into the sour cream mixture and chill.

When both are chilled, unmold mousse on a bed of fresh lettuce and pour the sauce over it.

Salmon And Cottage Cheese

1 pound salmon flesh, boned and skinned
½ cup milk
¼ cup butter or margarine
1 small onion
¼ cup all-purpose flour
Dash of tabasco sauce
Salt and pepper
1½ cups cottage cheese
Hot buttered biscuits or toast

Break the salmon into large pieces. Melt the butter in a saucepan. Chop the onion, and sauté the pieces until transparent but not browned. Blend in the flour, then add the milk to make a sauce. Cook over moderate heat, stirring constantly, until the sauce is thick and smooth. Add salt and pepper, and fold in the cottage cheese. Reduce the heat under the pan. Stirring gently, so as not to mash the cheese too much, fold in the salmon pieces. Reheat, and serve immediately on hot buttered biscuits or hot buttered toast.

16

Miscellaneous Salmon Dishes

Solianka (Russian Salmon Stew)

2 pounds salmon bones and heads
1½ quarts water
Salt and pepper
2 onions
4 dill pickles
3 large tomatoes
Oil
1 pound salmon flesh, boned, skinned and flaked
1 teaspoon capers
1 teaspoon chopped green olives
1 teaspoon chopped black olives
1 bay leaf
Parsley
4 tablespoons butter
Lemon slices

Prepare a bouillon with the heads and bones and water, well seasoned with salt and pepper. Peel the onions and chop them with the dill pickles. Peel, seed and chop the tomatoes and cook them in a little oil until they form a paste. Cut the salmon into strips and place them in a pan with the onion, pickles, tomato paste, capers, and chopped olives. Cover with the fish broth, which you have strained. Add the bay leaf and a sprig of parsley, and cook gently for 15 minutes. Add the butter. Serve in bowls garnished with chopped parsley, olives, and thin slices of lemon.

Maine-Style Salmon Chowder

1 pound salmon flesh, boned and skinned
1 chicken bouillon cube

1 cup boiling water
¾ cup chopped onion
½ cup chopped green pepper
1 clove garlic, finely chopped
¼ cup butter or other fat, melted
1/3 cup milk
1 pound can tomatoes
1 can (8 oz.) whole-kernel corn
1 cup sliced okra (optional)
½ teaspoon salt
¼ teaspoon thyme
¼ teaspoon pepper
1 whole bay leaf

Break salmon into large pieces. Dissolve bouillon cube in boiling water. Cook onion, green pepper, and garlic in butter until tender. Combine all ingredients and cook for 15 minutes or until vegetables are tender. Remove bay leaf. Serves six.

Part III
Sauces

California Sauce

2 tablespoons butter or margarine
2 tablespoons flour
½ teaspoon salt
½ teaspoon Ac'cent
4 tablespoons brown sugar
½ cup lemon juice
½ cup water
½ cup golden seedless raisins

Melt butter or margarine. Blend in flour, salt, Ac'cent and brown
sugar. Combine lemon juice and water, add to the rest, and stir
over a low flame until smooth and thickened. Add raisins and simmer for 5 minutes. Makes about 2 cups.

Thick White Sauce

3 tablespoons butter or fat
3 to 4 tablespoons flour
¼ teaspoon or more salt
1 cup milk, cream, or stock

Melt fat and remove from heat. Add flour and salt. Stir until
smooth. Add liquid gradually, stirring constantly over low heat
until mixture thickens.

Medium White Sauce

2 tablespoons butter or fat
2 tablespoons flour
¼ teaspoon salt
1 cup milk, cream, or stock

Melt fat and remove from heat. Add flour and salt. Stir until
smooth. Add liquid gradually, stirring constantly over low heat
until mixture thickens.

Cucumber Sauce

1 cup sour cream
½ cup seeded, grated cucumber
½ teaspoon salt
1 teaspoon finely chopped fresh dill
2 teaspoons chopped chives
½ teaspoon black pepper

Blend all the ingredients well. Allow the sauce to stand for 1 or 2 hours in the refrigerator before serving.

Mayonnaise Sauce

2 egg yolks
1 teaspoon salt
½ teaspoon dry mustard
1 pint peanut or olive oil
Lemon juice or vinegar

Beat the egg yolks, the salt and the mustard together and gradually add the oil, beating constantly until well thickened and stiff. Thin with lemon juice or vinegar to taste.

If the mayonnaise starts to curdle, begin over with another egg yolk and a little oil, and gradually add the curdled mixture. It is important to have the eggs and the oil at about the same temperature.

Sauce Verte (Green Mayonnaise Sauce)

To 2 cups of Mayonnaise Sauce, add 1 cup of mixed herbs (spinach, water cress, parsley, chives, tarragon) which have been chopped very fine—almost to a powder. Blend well.

Sauce Remoulade

2 cups mayonnaise
2 cloves garlic, finely chopped
1 tablespoon finely chopped tarragon
1 teaspoon dry mustard
2 hard-boiled eggs, finely chopped
1 tablespoon capers
1 tablespoon finely chopped parsley
1 teaspoon anchovy paste

Mix all the ingredients thoroughly and let stand for 2 hours before serving.

Sauce Velouté

2 tablespoons flour
2 tablespoons butter
1 cup fish stock
Salt and pepper

Combine the flour and butter and cook together until they are slightly browned or yellowish in color. Gradually stir in the fish stock, and continue stirring until it thickens. Cook 10 minutes and season to taste. This makes 1 cup of sauce.

It is customary, though not necessary, to add cream and egg yolks to this sauce. To 1 cup of sauce, add 1 cup of cream and 3 egg yolks. Beat the cream and egg yolks together well and gradually stir into the basic sauce. Continue stirring until the sauce is properly thickened and heated through. Be careful not let the mixture boil after the egg yolks have been added. This will increase your sauce to 2 cups.

Shrimp Sauce

To each cup of Sauce Velouté add ½ cup of finely chopped cooked shrimp.

Sauce À L'Americaine

3 tablespoons butter
1 chopped onion
6 chopped shallots, or green onions
5 ripe tomatoes, peeled, seeded and chopped
1 chopped clove of garlic
3 tablespoons chopped parsley
1 tablespoon chopped fresh tarragon, or 1 teaspoon
   dried tarragon
1½ teaspoons thyme
Salt and pepper
3 tablespoons tomato puree

Melt the butter and saute the onion for a few minutes. Add shallots, tomatoes, garlic and herbs and simmer for 1 hour. Season to taste and let cook down and blend thoroughly. Add the tomato puree at the last.

Sauce Béchamel

3 tablespoons sweet butter
2 small shallots, finely minced
3 tablespoons flour
2 cups milk
1½ cups clam juice
½ teaspoon salt

½ teaspoon black pepper
¼ teaspoon nutmeg

Melt butter in saucepan, stir in shallots and cook until soft. Add the flour, stir well and cook for 5 minutes. Do not let flour brown. Scald the milk, heat the clam broth and add these slowly, stirring and beating in a wire whisk. Stir in salt, pepper and nutmeg. Simmer for 25 minutes, stirring constantly. Sauce when finished will be smooth and creamy. This is excellent over poached fish, but is improved by turning it into Mustard Sauce or Caper Sauce.

Mustard Sauce

2 cups Sauce Béchamel
1½ teaspoons dry English mustard
1½ teaspoons water

Combine mustard and water and blend until smooth. Mix this into the 2 cups of Sauce Béchamel. Taste for tartness; if you want it sharper, make more mustard paste as described and stir it in.

Caper Sauce

2 cups Sauce Béchamel
½ cup capers, washed and drained
1 tablespoon freshly squeezed lemon juice
1½ teaspoons butter

Heat the Sauce Béchamel, add chopped capers, stir in lemon juice and butter, and blend well.

Austrian Almond Sauce

4 tablespoons butter
1 teaspoon large capers, drained and chopped
1 teaspoon slivered almonds
1 tablespoon freshly squeezed lemon juice

This sauce is good over any kind of fish, poached or otherwise. Melt the butter and blend in the capers, almonds and lemon juice. Simmer until very hot, stirring well. Spoon over fish.

Sauce Hollandaise

The three secrets to preparing a successful Hollandaise (sometimes called Sauce Isigny) are to use the finest of sweet butter, be sure the pan in which you make it does not touch the water below, and be certain that the water never boils. It is best to use a wire whisk.

3 egg yolks
1 or 2 teaspoons water
¼ pound (½ cup) butter, cut into small pieces
Few grains cayenne
Few grains salt
Lemon juice or tarragon vinegar

Combine the egg yolks and water in the upper part of a double boiler and whisk over hot water until the eggs are well mixed slightly thickened. Gradually add the butter. Whisk all the time, and be certain that the water below does not boil. If your sauce becomes too thick, dilute it with a little water. If it curdles, you can bring it back with a little boiling water. When it is properly emulsified, add the cayenne and a few grains of salt and the lemon juice (or vinegar) to taste.

Sauce Mousseline

One of the most delicate sauces in cookery, this is a combination of equal parts Sauce Hollandaise and whipped cream.

Sauce Béarnaise

½ cup tarragon vinegar
1/3 cup dry white wine
1 tablespoon finely chopped onion
½ teaspoon crushed, dried tarragon leaves
4 egg yolks
½ cup butter or margarine
Dash of salt
Dash of cayenne pepper

Place vinegar, wine, onion, and tarragon in a small saucepan. Bring to a boil over moderately low heat, and cook for 6 to 8 minutes, or until reduced to ½ cup. Strain and reserve liquid. Place egg yolks in top of a double boiler and beat slightly with a wire whisk or fork. Melt butter in saucepan over moderately low heat until just melted. Gradually add butter to egg yolks, mixing until blended. Gradually stir in wine mixture. Place over simmering, not boiling, water—water should not touch bottom of top pan —and cook until thickened, stirring constantly. Remove from heat and season with salt and cayenne. Makes about 1¼ cups.

Béarnaise Tomate

This is a blend of Sauce Béarnaise and tomato paste, flavored with a little salt and pepper and a bit of tarragon.

Sauce Tartare

1 cup mayonnaise or salad dressing
¼ cup drained sweet-pickle relish
1 tablespoon drained capers
1 tablespoon chopped parsley
2 teaspoons grated onion
1 teaspoon finely cut chives

Blend well in small bowl, cover and chill. Makes about 1⅓ cups.

Barbecue Sauce

2 medium onions, finely chopped
¼ cup olive oil
1 cup Italian tomato paste
1 teaspoon salt
1 teaspoon basil
½ cup steak sauce
¼ cup Worcestershire sauce
1 teaspoon dry mustard
½ cup strained honey
½ cup red wine

Saute the onions in olive oil until lightly browned. Add the tomato paste, salt, basil, steak sauce, Worcestershire sauce, mustard and honey. Allow to simmer for 5 minutes, stirring constantly. Add the wine and allow the sauce to come just to the boiling point. Taste for seasoning. Strain through a fine sieve.

Imperial Russian Sauce

2 cups mayonnaise
1 teaspoon dry mustard
2 tablespoons finely chopped onion
2 ounces caviar
1 tablespoon Worcestershire sauce

Blend well and let stand for 2 hours before serving.

Argentine Chuqui

The Traful River in Argentina is no doubt the greatest land-locked salmon water in the world today, so you can appreciate that the best possible basting sauce for salmon and trout also comes from Argentina. It is also good on game, and it will not blacken or burn, so it can be shaken liberally onto the cooking food all during the cooking process.

    2 onions, minced
    2 garlic cloves, minced
    2 teaspoons oregano or marjoram, or both
    2 bay leaves
    1 tablespoon salt
    1 teaspoon black pepper
    1 cup olive oil
    ½ cup vinegar
    ½ cup sherry

Saute the onions, garlic, herbs, salt and pepper in olive oil until the onions and garlic are well browned. Strain, saving the liquid and discarding the solid matter. This should leave you with 1 cup of liquid; if not, add enough additional olive oil to make 1 cup. Add the vinegar and sherry. Pour this into a bottle, such as a whiskey or beer bottle, and shake well. Plug the bottle with a tight-fitting cork with a hole in it. You may add more salt or 1 teaspoon of powdered mustard if you wish.

Index

Salmon

Sauces

Trout